The Jump Journal
Living a Life That Resonates

outcome publishing

Lakewood Ranch, Florida

THE JUMP JOURNAL: Living a Life That Resonates
by Tim Passmore

Published by Outcome Publishing
11523 Palm Brush Trail # 372
Lakewood Ranch, Florida 34202
www.outcomepublishing.com

This book or parts thereof may not be reproduced in any form, stored in a retrieval system, or transmitted in any form by any means – electronic, mechanical, photocopy, recording, or otherwise – without prior written permission of the publisher, except as provided by United States of America copyright law.

Unless otherwise indicated, Bible quotations are taken from The Holy Bible, New International Version. Copyright © 1973, 1978, 1984, by International Bible Society.

Copyright © 2010 by Tim Passmore
All rights reserved

First Edition

Printed in the United States of America

1. Religion: Spirituality General
2. Self-Help: Spiritual
3. Religion: Christian Life – Personal Growth

I seek you with all my heart; do not let me stray from your commands.
I have hidden your word in my heart that I might not sin against you.
Praise be to you, O LORD; teach me your decrees.

                                                          Psalm 119:10-12

Table of Contents

Introduction 7

The Journal 9

Group Takeaway Guides 271

Worship Takeaway Guides 325

Calendar 379

the jump journal

Introduction

What has God been saying to you lately? It's so awesome to know that God speaks to us and teaches us through His word. It's time to JUMP in and discover what God has to say to us about how to live an amazing life. I love what the psalmist wrote. Check it out!

> Blessed are they whose ways are blameless, who walk according to the law of the LORD. ^{2}Blessed are they who keep his statutes and seek him with all their heart... ^{10}I seek you with all my heart; do not let me stray from your commands. ^{11}I have hidden your word in my heart that I might not sin against you. ^{12}Praise be to you, O LORD; teach me your decrees. ^{13}With my lips I recount all the laws that come from your mouth. ^{14}I rejoice in following your statutes as one rejoices in great riches. ^{15}I meditate on your precepts and consider your ways. ^{16}I delight in your decrees; I will not neglect your word... ^{35}Direct me in the path of your commands, for there I find delight. ^{36}Turn my heart toward your statutes and not toward selfish gain. ^{37}Turn my eyes away from worthless things; preserve my life according to your word.
> Psalm 119:1-2, 10-16, 35-57

We are to hide God's Word in our hearts. What are you writing on the pages of your heart? We are to be writing the right things. Are you? The information that we take in has an affect on what we put out. This includes the actions we perform and the words we say. What do these things reveal about what you've written on the pages of your heart? Are you blameless, living up to the expectations God has for you? God wants us to turn our hearts toward Him and away from selfish things. He wants us to avoid trusting in things that are worthless and to know that we are of great worth. That's what He wants to say to you!

One way to write the right things is to allow God to speak to us through the study of His Word. We are to be passionate about hearing from Him. The psalmist had a heart that sought after God. He knew the blessings that come when we obey Him. Because of this, he knew the importance of knowing the expectations God has for us.

An important exercise in learning from God is to apply what He teaches to our lives. We are to measure who we are by what He says. We do this by allowing His words to speak to us. The psalmist wrote of our doing this when he said, *"I meditate on your precepts and consider your ways."* Are you considering His ways? How do we do it?

One way of making God's Word personal is to journal what He says to us. Applying God's teachings to life and writing them down engraves those things in our hearts. They become a filter through which we make decisions as we remember what He desires.

The purpose of this book is to help you discover what God wants to say to you. It's a tool to help you JUMP in to God's Word! Using it is very simple. There are guides in the section called "Quiet Time Guides" for you to use five times per week for fifty two weeks. You'll find on each guide the theme of a scripture along with the scripture passage you are to read. After reading, answer the questions and allow God to speak to you. For this to happen, you need to dedicate time to spend with Him and to give Him your full attention. Don't rush through in order to check it off of your "to do list" for the day. Make sure you clear your mind of your daily responsibilities and focus on Him. You'll be reading through the first half of the New Testament. Through the scriptures, you'll learn how to face challenges, trust in God, and make good choices each day.

You'll also find three other sections. Following the devotional guides there are "Group Takeaway" guides and "Worship Takeaway" guides. They are included to help you journal what you've learned through these learning experiences. Following this is a "Calendar" section for you to write upcoming events. These are events that you are planning to participate in that will help you learn more about God or serve Him.

That's it! Are your ready to get started? I hope that God will spiritually transform you as you listen to Him and learn from Him. God has a great plan for your future. Get pumped up about it because life is worth living!

LET'S JUMP IN!

quiet time guides

the jump journal

quiet time guides

one

Topic: The way prepared.

Scripture: Matthew 3:1-17

- **Summarize:** Summarize the Scripture in your own words.

- **Reflection:** What is God trying to teach you through this passage?

- **Key Verse:** What is the key verse that stands out to you as most important? Write it in the space provided.

- **Action:** What does God want you to do about what you have learned?

quiet time guides

two

Topic: Jesus tempted.

Scripture: Matthew 4:1-11

- **Summarize:** Summarize the Scripture in your own words.

- **Reflection:** What is God trying to teach you through this passage?

- **Key Verse:** What is the key verse that stands out to you as most important? Write it in the space provided.

- **Action:** What does God want you to do about what you have learned?

quiet time guides

1 three

Topic: Jesus preaching, calling and healing.

Scripture: Matthew 4:12-25

- **Summarize:** Summarize the Scripture in your own words.

- **Reflection:** What is God trying to teach you through this passage?

- **Key Verse:** What is the key verse that stands out to you as most important? Write it in the space provided.

- **Action:** What does God want you to do about what you have learned?

quiet time guides

four

Topic: The attitudes.

Scripture: Matthew 5:1-12

- **Summarize:** Summarize the Scripture in your own words.

- **Reflection:** What is God trying to teach you through this passage?

- **Key Verse:** What is the key verse that stands out to you as most important? Write it in the space provided.

- **Action:** What does God want you to do about what you have learned?

quiet time guides

1 *five*

Topic: Salt and light.

Scripture: Matthew 5:13-16

- **Summarize**: Summarize the Scripture in your own words.

- **Reflection**: What is God trying to teach you through this passage?

- **Key Verse**: What is the key verse that stands out to you as most important? Write it in the space provided.

- **Action**: What does God want you to do about what you have learned?

quiet time guides

2one

Topic: Living the righteous life.

Scripture: Matthew 5:17-20

- **Summarize:** Summarize the Scripture in your own words.

- **Reflection:** What is God trying to teach you through this passage?

- **Key Verse:** What is the key verse that stands out to you as most important? Write it in the space provided.

- **Action:** What does God want you to do about what you have learned?

quiet time guides

2 *two*

Topic: Dealing with anger.

Scripture: Matthew 5:21-26

- **Summarize**: Summarize the Scripture in your own words.

- **Reflection**: What is God trying to teach you through this passage?

- **Key Verse**: What is the key verse that stands out to you as most important? Write it in the space provided.

- **Action**: What does God want you to do about what you have learned?

quiet time guides

2three

Topic: Dealing with sin.

Scripture: Matthew 5:27-30

- **Summarize:** Summarize the Scripture in your own words.

- **Reflection:** What is God trying to teach you through this passage?

- **Key Verse:** What is the key verse that stands out to you as most important? Write it in the space provided.

- **Action:** What does God want you to do about what you have learned?

quiet time guides

four

Topic: Oaths, eyes and cheeks.

Scripture: Matthew 5:33-42

- **Summarize:** Summarize the Scripture in your own words.

- **Reflection:** What is God trying to teach you through this passage?

- **Key Verse:** What is the key verse that stands out to you as most important? Write it in the space provided.

- **Action:** What does God want you to do about what you have learned?

the jump journal

quiet time guides

2.five

Topic: Enemy loving.

Scripture: Matthew 5:43-48; Luke 6:27-36

- **Summarize:** Summarize the Scripture in your own words.

- **Reflection:** What is God trying to teach you through this passage?

- **Key Verse:** What is the key verse that stands out to you as most important? Write it in the space provided.

- **Action:** What does God want you to do about what you have learned?

quiet time guides

3 one

Topic: Giving to meet needs.

Scripture: Matthew 6:1-4

- **Summarize:** Summarize the Scripture in your own words.

- **Reflection:** What is God trying to teach you through this passage?

- **Key Verse:** What is the key verse that stands out to you as most important? Write it in the space provided.

- **Action:** What does God want you to do about what you have learned?

quiet time guides

3two

Topic: Prayer and fasting.

Scripture: Matthew 6:5-18; 9:14-17; Mark 1:35-39

- **Summarize:** Summarize the Scripture in your own words.

- **Reflection:** What is God trying to teach you through this passage?

- **Key Verse:** What is the key verse that stands out to you as most important? Write it in the space provided.

- **Action:** What does God want you to do about what you have learned?

quiet time guides

3three

Topic: Treasures.

Scripture: Matthew 6:19-24

- **Summarize:** Summarize the Scripture in your own words.

- **Reflection:** What is God trying to teach you through this passage?

- **Key Verse:** What is the key verse that stands out to you as most important? Write it in the space provided.

- **Action:** What does God want you to do about what you have learned?

quiet time guides

four

Topic: Anxiety.

Scripture: Matthew 6:25-34; 11:25-30; Luke 12:22-34

- **Summarize:** Summarize the Scripture in your own words.

- **Reflection:** What is God trying to teach you through this passage?

- **Key Verse:** What is the key verse that stands out to you as most important? Write it in the space provided.

- **Action:** What does God want you to do about what you have learned?

quiet time guides

3five

Topic: Judging.

Scripture: Matthew 7:1-6

- **Summarize:** Summarize the Scripture in your own words.

- **Reflection:** What is God trying to teach you through this passage?

- **Key Verse:** What is the key verse that stands out to you as most important? Write it in the space provided.

- **Action:** What does God want you to do about what you have learned?

quiet time guides

4 one

Topic: Asking, seeking and knocking.

Scripture: Matthew 7:7-12

- **Summarize:** Summarize the Scripture in your own words.

- **Reflection:** What is God trying to teach you through this passage?

- **Key Verse:** What is the key verse that stands out to you as most important? Write it in the space provided.

- **Action:** What does God want you to do about what you have learned?

the jump journal

quiet time guides

♃ *two*

Topic: The gates and the tree.

Scripture: Matthew 7:13-23; Luke 13:22-30

- **Summarize:** Summarize the Scripture in your own words.

- **Reflection:** What is God trying to teach you through this passage?

- **Key Verse:** What is the key verse that stands out to you as most important? Write it in the space provided.

- **Action:** What does God want you to do about what you have learned?

quiet time guides

4three

Topic: The builders.

Scripture: Matthew 7:24-29; Luke 6:46-49

- **Summarize:** Summarize the Scripture in your own words.

- **Reflection:** What is God trying to teach you through this passage?

- **Key Verse:** What is the key verse that stands out to you as most important? Write it in the space provided.

- **Action:** What does God want you to do about what you have learned?

quiet time guides

four

Topic: Healing.

Scripture: Matthew 8:1-17; 28-34

- **Summarize**: Summarize the Scripture in your own words.

- **Reflection**: What is God trying to teach you through this passage?

- **Key Verse**: What is the key verse that stands out to you as most important? Write it in the space provided.

- **Action**: What does God want you to do about what you have learned?

quiet time guides

♃five

Topic: Following and faith.

Scripture: Matthew 8:18-27; 21:18-22

- **Summarize:** Summarize the Scripture in your own words.

- **Reflection:** What is God trying to teach you through this passage?

- **Key Verse:** What is the key verse that stands out to you as most important? Write it in the space provided.

- **Action:** What does God want you to do about what you have learned?

quiet time guides

5 one

Topic: Forgiven.

Scripture: Matthew 9:1-8

- **Summarize:** Summarize the Scripture in your own words.

- **Reflection:** What is God trying to teach you through this passage?

- **Key Verse:** What is the key verse that stands out to you as most important? Write it in the space provided.

- **Action:** What does God want you to do about what you have learned?

quiet time guides

5two

Topic: The calling.

Scripture: Matthew 9:9-13

- **Summarize:** Summarize the Scripture in your own words.

- **Reflection:** What is God trying to teach you through this passage?

- **Key Verse:** What is the key verse that stands out to you as most important? Write it in the space provided.

- **Action:** What does God want you to do about what you have learned?

quiet time guides

5three

Topic: Faith and healing.

Scripture: Matthew 9:18-34

- **Summarize:** Summarize the Scripture in your own words.

- **Reflection:** What is God trying to teach you through this passage?

- **Key Verse:** What is the key verse that stands out to you as most important? Write it in the space provided.

- **Action:** What does God want you to do about what you have learned?

quiet time guides

5 four

Topic: The workers.

Scripture: Matthew 9:35-38

- **Summarize:** Summarize the Scripture in your own words.

- **Reflection:** What is God trying to teach you through this passage?

- **Key Verse:** What is the key verse that stands out to you as most important? Write it in the space provided.

- **Action:** What does God want you to do about what you have learned?

quiet time guides

5 *five*

Topic: A message to disciples.

Scripture: Matthew 10:1-10

- **Summarize**: Summarize the Scripture in your own words.

- **Reflection**: What is God trying to teach you through this passage?

- **Key Verse**: What is the key verse that stands out to you as most important? Write it in the space provided.

- **Action**: What does God want you to do about what you have learned?

quiet time guides

One

Topic: Jesus and John.

Scripture: Matthew 11:1-19

- **Summarize:** Summarize the Scripture in your own words.

- **Reflection:** What is God trying to teach you through this passage?

- **Key Verse:** What is the key verse that stands out to you as most important? Write it in the space provided.

- **Action:** What does God want you to do about what you have learned?

quiet time guides

6two

Topic: The Sabbath and the servant.

Scripture: Matthew 12:1-21

- **Summarize:** Summarize the Scripture in your own words.

- **Reflection:** What is God trying to teach you through this passage?

- **Key Verse:** What is the key verse that stands out to you as most important? Write it in the space provided.

- **Action:** What does God want you to do about what you have learned?

quiet time guides

three

Topic: Divided kingdoms.

Scripture: Matthew 12:22-37

- **Summarize:** Summarize the Scripture in your own words.

- **Reflection:** What is God trying to teach you through this passage?

- **Key Verse:** What is the key verse that stands out to you as most important? Write it in the space provided.

- **Action:** What does God want you to do about what you have learned?

quiet time guides

four

Topic: Jonah.

Scripture: Matthew 12:38-45

- **Summarize**: Summarize the Scripture in your own words.

- **Reflection**: What is God trying to teach you through this passage?

- **Key Verse**: What is the key verse that stands out to you as most important? Write it in the space provided.

- **Action**: What does God want you to do about what you have learned?

quiet time guides

five

Topic: The sower.

Scripture: Matthew 13:1-23

- **Summarize:** Summarize the Scripture in your own words.

- **Reflection:** What is God trying to teach you through this passage?

- **Key Verse:** What is the key verse that stands out to you as most important? Write it in the space provided.

- **Action:** What does God want you to do about what you have learned?

quiet time guides

Zone

Topic: Weeds.

Scripture: Matthew 13:24-30

- **Summarize:** Summarize the Scripture in your own words.

- **Reflection:** What is God trying to teach you through this passage?

- **Key Verse:** What is the key verse that stands out to you as most important? Write it in the space provided.

- **Action:** What does God want you to do about what you have learned?

quiet time guides

two

Topic: The mustard seed.

Scripture: Matthew 13:31-43

- **Summarize:** Summarize the Scripture in your own words.

- **Reflection:** What is God trying to teach you through this passage?

- **Key Verse:** What is the key verse that stands out to you as most important? Write it in the space provided.

- **Action:** What does God want you to do about what you have learned?

quiet time guides

three

Topic: The treasure and the net.

Scripture: Matthew 13:44-52

- **Summarize:** Summarize the Scripture in your own words.

- **Reflection:** What is God trying to teach you through this passage?

- **Key Verse:** What is the key verse that stands out to you as most important? Write it in the space provided.

- **Action:** What does God want you to do about what you have learned?

quiet time guides

four

Topic: Miracles.

Scripture: Matthew 14:13-36; 15:29-39; 20:29-34

- **Summarize:** Summarize the Scripture in your own words.

- **Reflection:** What is God trying to teach you through this passage?

- **Key Verse:** What is the key verse that stands out to you as most important? Write it in the space provided.

- **Action:** What does God want you to do about what you have learned?

quiet time guides

𝓉 *five*

Topic: Clean and unclean.

Scripture: Matthew 15:1-20

- **Summarize:** Summarize the Scripture in your own words.

- **Reflection:** What is God trying to teach you through this passage?

- **Key Verse:** What is the key verse that stands out to you as most important? Write it in the space provided.

- **Action:** What does God want you to do about what you have learned?

quiet time guides

8 one

Topic: Signs, yeast, confession and death.

Scripture: Matthew 16:1-28

- **Summarize:** Summarize the Scripture in your own words.

- **Reflection:** What is God trying to teach you through this passage?

- **Key Verse:** What is the key verse that stands out to you as most important? Write it in the space provided.

- **Action:** What does God want you to do about what you have learned?

quiet time guides

8two

Topic: Transfigured.

Scripture: Matthew 17:1-23

- **Summarize:** Summarize the Scripture in your own words.

- **Reflection:** What is God trying to teach you through this passage?

- **Key Verse:** What is the key verse that stands out to you as most important? Write it in the space provided.

- **Action:** What does God want you to do about what you have learned?

quiet time guides

8three

Topic: The greatest.

Scripture: Matthew 18:1-9; 20:20-28

- **Summarize:** Summarize the Scripture in your own words.

- **Reflection:** What is God trying to teach you through this passage?

- **Key Verse:** What is the key verse that stands out to you as most important? Write it in the space provided.

- **Action:** What does God want you to do about what you have learned?

quiet time guides

four

Topic: The lost sheep and the sinner.

Scripture: Matthew 18:10-20; Luke 15:1-7

- **Summarize:** Summarize the Scripture in your own words.

- **Reflection:** What is God trying to teach you through this passage?

- **Key Verse:** What is the key verse that stands out to you as most important? Write it in the space provided.

- **Action:** What does God want you to do about what you have learned?

quiet time guides

five

Topic: A servant problem.

Scripture: Matthew 18:21-35

- **Summarize:** Summarize the Scripture in your own words.

- **Reflection:** What is God trying to teach you through this passage?

- **Key Verse:** What is the key verse that stands out to you as most important? Write it in the space provided.

- **Action:** What does God want you to do about what you have learned?

quiet time guides

One

Topic: Little children and a rich man.

Scripture: Matthew 19:13-30

- **Summarize:** Summarize the Scripture in your own words.

- **Reflection:** What is God trying to teach you through this passage?

- **Key Verse:** What is the key verse that stands out to you as most important? Write it in the space provided.

- **Action:** What does God want you to do about what you have learned?

quiet time guides

9two

Topic: The vineyard.

Scripture: Matthew 20:1-16

- **Summarize:** Summarize the Scripture in your own words.

- **Reflection:** What is God trying to teach you through this passage?

- **Key Verse:** What is the key verse that stands out to you as most important? Write it in the space provided.

- **Action:** What does God want you to do about what you have learned?

quiet time guides

three

Topic: Two sons and the tenants.

Scripture: Matthew 21:28-46

- **Summarize:** Summarize the Scripture in your own words.

- **Reflection:** What is God trying to teach you through this passage?

- **Key Verse:** What is the key verse that stands out to you as most important? Write it in the space provided.

- **Action:** What does God want you to do about what you have learned?

quiet time guides

four

Topic: The wedding banquet.

Scripture: Matthew 22:1-14

- **Summarize**: Summarize the Scripture in your own words.

- **Reflection**: What is God trying to teach you through this passage?

- **Key Verse**: What is the key verse that stands out to you as most important? Write it in the space provided.

- **Action**: What does God want you to do about what you have learned?

quiet time guides

five

Topic: The love command.

Scripture: Matthew 22:34-40

- **Summarize:** Summarize the Scripture in your own words.

- **Reflection:** What is God trying to teach you through this passage?

- **Key Verse:** What is the key verse that stands out to you as most important? Write it in the space provided.

- **Action:** What does God want you to do about what you have learned?

quiet time guides

10 one

Topic: Woes.

Scripture: Matthew 23:1-39

- **Summarize:** Summarize the Scripture in your own words.

- **Reflection:** What is God trying to teach you through this passage?

- **Key Verse:** What is the key verse that stands out to you as most important? Write it in the space provided.

- **Action:** What does God want you to do about what you have learned?

quiet time guides

10*two*

Topic: The end signs.

Scripture: Matthew 24:1-35

- **Summarize:** Summarize the Scripture in your own words.

- **Reflection:** What is God trying to teach you through this passage?

- **Key Verse:** What is the key verse that stands out to you as most important? Write it in the space provided.

- **Action:** What does God want you to do about what you have learned?

quiet time guides

10 three

Topic: The unknown time.

Scripture: Matthew 24:36-51

- **Summarize:** Summarize the Scripture in your own words.

- **Reflection:** What is God trying to teach you through this passage?

- **Key Verse:** What is the key verse that stands out to you as most important? Write it in the space provided.

- **Action:** What does God want you to do about what you have learned?

quiet time guides

10 four

Topic: Ten virgins and talents.

Scripture: Matthew 25:1-30

- **Summarize:** Summarize the Scripture in your own words.

- **Reflection:** What is God trying to teach you through this passage?

- **Key Verse:** What is the key verse that stands out to you as most important? Write it in the space provided.

- **Action:** What does God want you to do about what you have learned?

quiet time guides

10 five

Topic: Sheep and goats.

Scripture: Matthew 25:31-46

- **Summarize:** Summarize the Scripture in your own words.

- **Reflection:** What is God trying to teach you through this passage?

- **Key Verse:** What is the key verse that stands out to you as most important? Write it in the space provided.

- **Action:** What does God want you to do about what you have learned?

quiet time guides

11 one

Topic: The Lord's Supper.

Scripture: Matthew 26:17-30

- **Summarize:** Summarize the Scripture in your own words.

- **Reflection:** What is God trying to teach you through this passage?

- **Key Verse:** What is the key verse that stands out to you as most important? Write it in the space provided.

- **Action:** What does God want you to do about what you have learned?

quiet time guides

11 *two*

Topic: Denial and prayer.

Scripture: Matthew 26:31-46, 69-75

- **Summarize:** Summarize the Scripture in your own words.

- **Reflection:** What is God trying to teach you through this passage?

- **Key Verse:** What is the key verse that stands out to you as most important? Write it in the space provided.

- **Action:** What does God want you to do about what you have learned?

quiet time guides

11 *three*

Topic: Crucifixion.

Scripture: Matthew 27:1-65

- **Summarize**: Summarize the Scripture in your own words.

- **Reflection**: What is God trying to teach you through this passage?

- **Key Verse**: What is the key verse that stands out to you as most important? Write it in the space provided.

- **Action**: What does God want you to do about what you have learned?

quiet time guides

11 *four*

Topic: Resurrection.

Scripture: Matthew 28:1-15

- **Summarize:** Summarize the Scripture in your own words.

- **Reflection:** What is God trying to teach you through this passage?

- **Key Verse:** What is the key verse that stands out to you as most important? Write it in the space provided.

- **Action:** What does God want you to do about what you have learned?

quiet time guides

11 *five*

Topic: The commission.

Scripture: Matthew 28:16-20

- **Summarize:** Summarize the Scripture in your own words.

- **Reflection:** What is God trying to teach you through this passage?

- **Key Verse:** What is the key verse that stands out to you as most important? Write it in the space provided.

- **Action:** What does God want you to do about what you have learned?

quiet time guides

12 one

Topic: Called.

Scripture: Mark 1:14-20

- **Summarize:** Summarize the Scripture in your own words.

- **Reflection:** What is God trying to teach you through this passage?

- **Key Verse:** What is the key verse that stands out to you as most important? Write it in the space provided.

- **Action:** What does God want you to do about what you have learned?

quiet time guides

12*two*

Topic: Needing a doctor.

Scripture: Mark 2:13-22

- **Summarize:** Summarize the Scripture in your own words.

- **Reflection:** What is God trying to teach you through this passage?

- **Key Verse:** What is the key verse that stands out to you as most important? Write it in the space provided.

- **Action:** What does God want you to do about what you have learned?

quiet time guides

12 three

Topic: A lamp stand and a growing seed.

Scripture: Mark 4:21-29

- **Summarize:** Summarize the Scripture in your own words.

- **Reflection:** What is God trying to teach you through this passage?

- **Key Verse:** What is the key verse that stands out to you as most important? Write it in the space provided.

- **Action:** What does God want you to do about what you have learned?

quiet time guides

12 four

Topic: Peter's confession.

Scripture: Mark 8:27-9:1

- **Summarize:** Summarize the Scripture in your own words.

- **Reflection:** What is God trying to teach you through this passage?

- **Key Verse:** What is the key verse that stands out to you as most important? Write it in the space provided.

- **Action:** What does God want you to do about what you have learned?

quiet time guides

12 five

Topic: Bad influences.

Scripture: Mark 9:42-50

- **Summarize:** Summarize the Scripture in your own words.

- **Reflection:** What is God trying to teach you through this passage?

- **Key Verse:** What is the key verse that stands out to you as most important? Write it in the space provided.

- **Action:** What does God want you to do about what you have learned?

quiet time guides

13 one

Topic: Teachers and an offering.

Scripture: Mark 12:35-44

- **Summarize**: Summarize the Scripture in your own words.

- **Reflection**: What is God trying to teach you through this passage?

- **Key Verse**: What is the key verse that stands out to you as most important? Write it in the space provided.

- **Action**: What does God want you to do about what you have learned?

quiet time guides

13*two*

Topic: The temptation.

Scripture: Luke 4:1-13

- **Summarize:** Summarize the Scripture in your own words.

- **Reflection:** What is God trying to teach you through this passage?

- **Key Verse:** What is the key verse that stands out to you as most important? Write it in the space provided.

- **Action:** What does God want you to do about what you have learned?

quiet time guides

13 *three*

Topic: Rejected.

Scripture: Luke 4:14-30

- **Summarize:** Summarize the Scripture in your own words.

- **Reflection:** What is God trying to teach you through this passage?

- **Key Verse:** What is the key verse that stands out to you as most important? Write it in the space provided.

- **Action:** What does God want you to do about what you have learned?

quiet time guides

13 four

Topic: "72"

Scripture: Luke 10:1-24

- **Summarize:** Summarize the Scripture in your own words.

- **Reflection:** What is God trying to teach you through this passage?

- **Key Verse:** What is the key verse that stands out to you as most important? Write it in the space provided.

- **Action:** What does God want you to do about what you have learned?

quiet time guides

13 five

Topic: Good Samaritan.

Scripture: Luke 10:25-37

- **Summarize:** Summarize the Scripture in your own words.

- **Reflection:** What is God trying to teach you through this passage?

- **Key Verse:** What is the key verse that stands out to you as most important? Write it in the space provided.

- **Action:** What does God want you to do about what you have learned?

quiet time guides

14 one

Topic: Six Woes.

Scripture: Luke 11:37-53

- **Summarize:** Summarize the Scripture in your own words.

- **Reflection:** What is God trying to teach you through this passage?

- **Key Verse:** What is the key verse that stands out to you as most important? Write it in the space provided.

- **Action:** What does God want you to do about what you have learned?

quiet time guides

14 *two*

Topic: Warnings and a fool.

Scripture: Luke 12:1-21

- **Summarize:** Summarize the Scripture in your own words.

- **Reflection:** What is God trying to teach you through this passage?

- **Key Verse:** What is the key verse that stands out to you as most important? Write it in the space provided.

- **Action:** What does God want you to do about what you have learned?

quiet time guides

14 three

Topic: Ready to serve.

Scripture: Luke 12:35-48

- **Summarize:** Summarize the Scripture in your own words.

- **Reflection:** What is God trying to teach you through this passage?

- **Key Verse:** What is the key verse that stands out to you as most important? Write it in the space provided.

- **Action:** What does God want you to do about what you have learned?

quiet time guides

14 four

Topic: Repenting or perishing.

Scripture: Luke 13:10-17

- **Summarize:** Summarize the Scripture in your own words.

- **Reflection:** What is God trying to teach you through this passage?

- **Key Verse:** What is the key verse that stands out to you as most important? Write it in the space provided.

- **Action:** What does God want you to do about what you have learned?

quiet time guides

14 five

Topic: Caring for a city.

Scripture: Luke 13 31-35

- **Summarize:** Summarize the Scripture in your own words.

- **Reflection:** What is God trying to teach you through this passage?

- **Key Verse:** What is the key verse that stands out to you as most important? Write it in the space provided.

- **Action:** What does God want you to do about what you have learned?

quiet time guides

15 one

Topic: A Pharisees house.

Scripture: Luke 14:1-14

- **Summarize:** Summarize the Scripture in your own words.

- **Reflection:** What is God trying to teach you through this passage?

- **Key Verse:** What is the key verse that stands out to you as most important? Write it in the space provided.

- **Action:** What does God want you to do about what you have learned?

quiet time guides

15 *two*

Topic: An awesome banquet.

Scripture: Luke 14:15-24

- **Summarize:** Summarize the Scripture in your own words.

- **Reflection:** What is God trying to teach you through this passage?

- **Key Verse:** What is the key verse that stands out to you as most important? Write it in the space provided.

- **Action:** What does God want you to do about what you have learned?

quiet time guides

15 three

Topic: The cost.

Scripture: Luke 14:25-35

- **Summarize:** Summarize the Scripture in your own words.

- **Reflection:** What is God trying to teach you through this passage?

- **Key Verse:** What is the key verse that stands out to you as most important? Write it in the space provided.

- **Action:** What does God want you to do about what you have learned?

the jump journal

quiet time guides

15 four

Topic: The lost son.

Scripture: Luke 15:11-32

- **Summarize:** Summarize the Scripture in your own words.

- **Reflection:** What is God trying to teach you through this passage?

- **Key Verse:** What is the key verse that stands out to you as most important? Write it in the space provided.

- **Action:** What does God want you to do about what you have learned?

quiet time guides

15 five

Topic: The shrewd manager.

Scripture: Luke 16:1-15

- **Summarize:** Summarize the Scripture in your own words.

- **Reflection:** What is God trying to teach you through this passage?

- **Key Verse:** What is the key verse that stands out to you as most important? Write it in the space provided.

- **Action:** What does God want you to do about what you have learned?

quiet time guides

16one

Topic: The rich guy and Lazarus.

Scripture: Luke 16:19-31

- **Summarize:** Summarize the Scripture in your own words.

- **Reflection:** What is God trying to teach you through this passage?

- **Key Verse:** What is the key verse that stands out to you as most important? Write it in the space provided.

- **Action:** What does God want you to do about what you have learned?

quiet time guides

16*two*

Topic: Sin spreader.

Scripture: Luke 17:1-10

- **Summarize**: Summarize the Scripture in your own words.

- **Reflection**: What is God trying to teach you through this passage?

- **Key Verse**: What is the key verse that stands out to you as most important? Write it in the space provided.

- **Action**: What does God want you to do about what you have learned?

quiet time guides

16 three

Topic: Healing the 10.

Scripture: Luke 17:11-19

- **Summarize:** Summarize the Scripture in your own words.

- **Reflection:** What is God trying to teach you through this passage?

- **Key Verse:** What is the key verse that stands out to you as most important? Write it in the space provided.

- **Action:** What does God want you to do about what you have learned?

the jump journal

quiet time guides

16 four

Topic: The coming kingdom.

Scripture: Luke 17:20-37

- **Summarize:** Summarize the Scripture in your own words.

- **Reflection:** What is God trying to teach you through this passage?

- **Key Verse:** What is the key verse that stands out to you as most important? Write it in the space provided.

- **Action:** What does God want you to do about what you have learned?

quiet time guides

16 five

Topic: The persistent widow.

Scripture: Luke 18:1-8

- **Summarize:** Summarize the Scripture in your own words.

- **Reflection:** What is God trying to teach you through this passage?

- **Key Verse:** What is the key verse that stands out to you as most important? Write it in the space provided.

- **Action:** What does God want you to do about what you have learned?

quiet time guides

17 one

Topic: A Pharisee and a tax collector.

Scripture: Luke 18:9-14

- **Summarize:** Summarize the Scripture in your own words.

- **Reflection:** What is God trying to teach you through this passage?

- **Key Verse:** What is the key verse that stands out to you as most important? Write it in the space provided.

- **Action:** What does God want you to do about what you have learned?

quiet time guides

17 *two*

Topic: Little children and rich ruler.

Scripture: Luke 18:15-30

- **Summarize:** Summarize the Scripture in your own words.

- **Reflection:** What is God trying to teach you through this passage?

- **Key Verse:** What is the key verse that stands out to you as most important? Write it in the space provided.

- **Action:** What does God want you to do about what you have learned?

the jump journal

quiet time guides

17 three

Topic: A beggar and his sight.

Scripture: Luke 18:35-43

- **Summarize:** Summarize the Scripture in your own words.

- **Reflection:** What is God trying to teach you through this passage?

- **Key Verse:** What is the key verse that stands out to you as most important? Write it in the space provided.

- **Action:** What does God want you to do about what you have learned?

quiet time guides

17 four

Topic: Zacchaeus.

Scripture: Luke 19:1-10

- **Summarize:** Summarize the Scripture in your own words.

- **Reflection:** What is God trying to teach you through this passage?

- **Key Verse:** What is the key verse that stands out to you as most important? Write it in the space provided.

- **Action:** What does God want you to do about what you have learned?

quiet time guides

17 five

Topic: Investment.

Scripture: Luke 19:11-27

- **Summarize:** Summarize the Scripture in your own words.

- **Reflection:** What is God trying to teach you through this passage?

- **Key Verse:** What is the key verse that stands out to you as most important? Write it in the space provided.

- **Action:** What does God want you to do about what you have learned?

18 one

Topic: The entry.

Scripture: Luke 19:28-44

- **Summarize:** Summarize the Scripture in your own words.

- **Reflection:** What is God trying to teach you through this passage?

- **Key Verse:** What is the key verse that stands out to you as most important? Write it in the space provided.

- **Action:** What does God want you to do about what you have learned?

quiet time guides

18 *two*

Topic: Tax paying.

Scripture: Luke 20:20-26

- **Summarize:** Summarize the Scripture in your own words.

- **Reflection:** What is God trying to teach you through this passage?

- **Key Verse:** What is the key verse that stands out to you as most important? Write it in the space provided.

- **Action:** What does God want you to do about what you have learned?

the jump journal

quiet time guides

18three

Topic: Resurrection and marriage.

Scripture: Luke 20:27-40

- **Summarize:** Summarize the Scripture in your own words.

- **Reflection:** What is God trying to teach you through this passage?

- **Key Verse:** What is the key verse that stands out to you as most important? Write it in the space provided.

- **Action:** What does God want you to do about what you have learned?

quiet time guides

18 four

Topic: Beware of the teachers.

Scripture: Luke 20:41-47

- **Summarize:** Summarize the Scripture in your own words.

- **Reflection:** What is God trying to teach you through this passage?

- **Key Verse:** What is the key verse that stands out to you as most important? Write it in the space provided.

- **Action:** What does God want you to do about what you have learned?

the jump journal

quiet time guides

18 *five*

Topic: Sign of the end.

Scripture: Luke 21:5-38

- **Summarize:** Summarize the Scripture in your own words.

- **Reflection:** What is God trying to teach you through this passage?

- **Key Verse:** What is the key verse that stands out to you as most important? Write it in the space provided.

- **Action:** What does God want you to do about what you have learned?

quiet time guides

19 one

Topic: The Last Supper.

Scripture: Luke 22:7-38

- **Summarize:** Summarize the Scripture in your own words.

- **Reflection:** What is God trying to teach you through this passage?

- **Key Verse:** What is the key verse that stands out to you as most important? Write it in the space provided.

- **Action:** What does God want you to do about what you have learned?

quiet time guides

19*two*

Topic: A prayer by Jesus.

Scripture: Luke 22:39-46

- **Summarize:** Summarize the Scripture in your own words.

- **Reflection:** What is God trying to teach you through this passage?

- **Key Verse:** What is the key verse that stands out to you as most important? Write it in the space provided.

- **Action:** What does God want you to do about what you have learned?

quiet time guides

19 three

Topic: Disowned.

Scripture: Luke 22:54-71

- **Summarize:** Summarize the Scripture in your own words.

- **Reflection:** What is God trying to teach you through this passage?

- **Key Verse:** What is the key verse that stands out to you as most important? Write it in the space provided.

- **Action:** What does God want you to do about what you have learned?

quiet time guides

19 four

Topic: The Crucifixion.

Scripture: Luke 23:26-43

- **Summarize:** Summarize the Scripture in your own words.

- **Reflection:** What is God trying to teach you through this passage?

- **Key Verse:** What is the key verse that stands out to you as most important? Write it in the space provided.

- **Action:** What does God want you to do about what you have learned?

quiet time guides

19 *five*

Topic: Death and Resurrection.

Scripture: Luke 23:44 - 24:12

- **Summarize:** Summarize the Scripture in your own words.

- **Reflection:** What is God trying to teach you through this passage?

- **Key Verse:** What is the key verse that stands out to you as most important? Write it in the space provided.

- **Action:** What does God want you to do about what you have learned?

quiet time guides

20 one

Topic: On the road.

Scripture: Luke 24:13-35

- **Summarize:** Summarize the Scripture in your own words.

- **Reflection:** What is God trying to teach you through this passage?

- **Key Verse:** What is the key verse that stands out to you as most important? Write it in the space provided.

- **Action:** What does God want you to do about what you have learned?

quiet time guides

20 two

Topic: The appearing.

Scripture: Luke 24:36-53

- **Summarize:** Summarize the Scripture in your own words.

- **Reflection:** What is God trying to teach you through this passage?

- **Key Verse:** What is the key verse that stands out to you as most important? Write it in the space provided.

- **Action:** What does God want you to do about what you have learned?

ns of n
quiet time guides

20three

Topic: The Word in the flesh.

Scripture: John 1:1-18

- **Summarize:** Summarize the Scripture in your own words.

- **Reflection:** What is God trying to teach you through this passage?

- **Key Verse:** What is the key verse that stands out to you as most important? Write it in the space provided.

- **Action:** What does God want you to do about what you have learned?

quiet time guides

20 four

Topic: The Lamb of God.

Scripture: John 1:29-42

- **Summarize:** Summarize the Scripture in your own words.

- **Reflection:** What is God trying to teach you through this passage?

- **Key Verse:** What is the key verse that stands out to you as most important? Write it in the space provided.

- **Action:** What does God want you to do about what you have learned?

quiet time guides

20 *five*

Topic: Phillip and Nathanael.

Scripture: John 1:43-51

- **Summarize:** Summarize the Scripture in your own words.

- **Reflection:** What is God trying to teach you through this passage?

- **Key Verse:** What is the key verse that stands out to you as most important? Write it in the space provided.

- **Action:** What does God want you to do about what you have learned?

quiet time guides

21 one

Topic: Water into wine.

Scripture: John 2:1-11

- **Summarize:** Summarize the Scripture in your own words.

- **Reflection:** What is God trying to teach you through this passage?

- **Key Verse:** What is the key verse that stands out to you as most important? Write it in the space provided.

- **Action:** What does God want you to do about what you have learned?

quiet time guides

21 *two*

Topic: Clearing the temple.

Scripture: John 2:12-25

- **Summarize:** Summarize the Scripture in your own words.

- **Reflection:** What is God trying to teach you through this passage?

- **Key Verse:** What is the key verse that stands out to you as most important? Write it in the space provided.

- **Action:** What does God want you to do about what you have learned?

quiet time guides

21 *three*

Topic: Teaching Nicodemus.

Scripture: John 3:1-21

- **Summarize:** Summarize the Scripture in your own words.

- **Reflection:** What is God trying to teach you through this passage?

- **Key Verse:** What is the key verse that stands out to you as most important? Write it in the space provided.

- **Action:** What does God want you to do about what you have learned?

the jump journal

quiet time guides

21 four

Topic: Testimony about Jesus.

Scripture: John 3:22-36

- **Summarize:** Summarize the Scripture in your own words.

- **Reflection:** What is God trying to teach you through this passage?

- **Key Verse:** What is the key verse that stands out to you as most important? Write it in the space provided.

- **Action:** What does God want you to do about what you have learned?

quiet time guides

21 *five*

Topic: A conversation with a woman.

Scripture: John 4:1-26

- **Summarize:** Summarize the Scripture in your own words.

- **Reflection:** What is God trying to teach you through this passage?

- **Key Verse:** What is the key verse that stands out to you as most important? Write it in the space provided.

- **Action:** What does God want you to do about what you have learned?

quiet time guides

22 one

Topic: "My food."

Scripture: John 4:27-38

- **Summarize:** Summarize the Scripture in your own words.

- **Reflection:** What is God trying to teach you through this passage?

- **Key Verse:** What is the key verse that stands out to you as most important? Write it in the space provided.

- **Action:** What does God want you to do about what you have learned?

quiet time guides

22 *two*

Topic: Healing the son.

Scripture: John 4:43-54

- **Summarize:** Summarize the Scripture in your own words.

- **Reflection:** What is God trying to teach you through this passage?

- **Key Verse:** What is the key verse that stands out to you as most important? Write it in the space provided.

- **Action:** What does God want you to do about what you have learned?

quiet time guides

22*three*

Topic: Healing at the pool.

Scripture: John 5:1-15

- **Summarize:** Summarize the Scripture in your own words.

- **Reflection:** What is God trying to teach you through this passage?

- **Key Verse:** What is the key verse that stands out to you as most important? Write it in the space provided.

- **Action:** What does God want you to do about what you have learned?

quiet time guides

22 four

Topic: Life through the Son.

Scripture: John 5:16-30

- **Summarize:** Summarize the Scripture in your own words.

- **Reflection:** What is God trying to teach you through this passage?

- **Key Verse:** What is the key verse that stands out to you as most important? Write it in the space provided.

- **Action:** What does God want you to do about what you have learned?

the jump journal

quiet time guides

22 five

Topic: Testimonies.

Scripture: John 5:31-47

- **Summarize:** Summarize the Scripture in your own words.

- **Reflection:** What is God trying to teach you through this passage?

- **Key Verse:** What is the key verse that stands out to you as most important? Write it in the space provided.

- **Action:** What does God want you to do about what you have learned?

quiet time guides

23 one

Topic: Walking on water.

Scripture: John 6:16-24

- **Summarize:** Summarize the Scripture in your own words.

- **Reflection:** What is God trying to teach you through this passage?

- **Key Verse:** What is the key verse that stands out to you as most important? Write it in the space provided.

- **Action:** What does God want you to do about what you have learned?

quiet time guides

23 *two*

Topic: The Bread of Life.

Scripture: John 6:25-40

- **Summarize:** Summarize the Scripture in your own words.

- **Reflection:** What is God trying to teach you through this passage?

- **Key Verse:** What is the key verse that stands out to you as most important? Write it in the space provided.

- **Action:** What does God want you to do about what you have learned?

quiet time guides

23 three

Topic: More about bread.

Scripture: John 6:41-59

- **Summarize:** Summarize the Scripture in your own words.

- **Reflection:** What is God trying to teach you through this passage?

- **Key Verse:** What is the key verse that stands out to you as most important? Write it in the space provided.

- **Action:** What does God want you to do about what you have learned?

quiet time guides

23 four

Topic: Deserters.

Scripture: John 6:60-71

- **Summarize:** Summarize the Scripture in your own words.

- **Reflection:** What is God trying to teach you through this passage?

- **Key Verse:** What is the key verse that stands out to you as most important? Write it in the space provided.

- **Action:** What does God want you to do about what you have learned?

quiet time guides

23 five

Topic: A feast.

Scripture: John 7:1-13

- **Summarize:** Summarize the Scripture in your own words.

- **Reflection:** What is God trying to teach you through this passage?

- **Key Verse:** What is the key verse that stands out to you as most important? Write it in the space provided.

- **Action:** What does God want you to do about what you have learned?

quiet time guides

24 one

Topic: The teaching.

Scripture: John 7:14-24

- **Summarize:** Summarize the Scripture in your own words.

- **Reflection:** What is God trying to teach you through this passage?

- **Key Verse:** What is the key verse that stands out to you as most important? Write it in the space provided.

- **Action:** What does God want you to do about what you have learned?

quiet time guides

24 *two*

Topic: The question.

Scripture: John 7:25-44

- **Summarize:** Summarize the Scripture in your own words.

- **Reflection:** What is God trying to teach you through this passage?

- **Key Verse:** What is the key verse that stands out to you as most important? Write it in the space provided.

- **Action:** What does God want you to do about what you have learned?

quiet time guides

24 three

Topic: A valid testimony.

Scripture: John 8:12-30

- **Summarize:** Summarize the Scripture in your own words.

- **Reflection:** What is God trying to teach you through this passage?

- **Key Verse:** What is the key verse that stands out to you as most important? Write it in the space provided.

- **Action:** What does God want you to do about what you have learned?

quiet time guides

24 four

Topic: Abraham's testimony.

Scripture: John 8:31-41

- **Summarize:** Summarize the Scripture in your own words.

- **Reflection:** What is God trying to teach you through this passage?

- **Key Verse:** What is the key verse that stands out to you as most important? Write it in the space provided.

- **Action:** What does God want you to do about what you have learned?

quiet time guides

24 five

Topic: The Devil's children.

Scripture: John 8:42-47

- **Summarize:** Summarize the Scripture in your own words.

- **Reflection:** What is God trying to teach you through this passage?

- **Key Verse:** What is the key verse that stands out to you as most important? Write it in the space provided.

- **Action:** What does God want you to do about what you have learned?

quiet time guides

25one

Topic: Claims.

Scripture: John 8:48-59

- **Summarize:** Summarize the Scripture in your own words.

- **Reflection:** What is God trying to teach you through this passage?

- **Key Verse:** What is the key verse that stands out to you as most important? Write it in the space provided.

- **Action:** What does God want you to do about what you have learned?

quiet time guides

25*two*

Topic: The man born blind.

Scripture: John 9:1-12

- **Summarize:** Summarize the Scripture in your own words.

- **Reflection:** What is God trying to teach you through this passage?

- **Key Verse:** What is the key verse that stands out to you as most important? Write it in the space provided.

- **Action:** What does God want you to do about what you have learned?

quiet time guides

25 three

Topic: Spiritual blindness.

Scripture: John 9:35-41

- **Summarize:** Summarize the Scripture in your own words.

- **Reflection:** What is God trying to teach you through this passage?

- **Key Verse:** What is the key verse that stands out to you as most important? Write it in the space provided.

- **Action:** What does God want you to do about what you have learned?

/ # quiet time guides

25four

Topic: The flock.

Scripture: John 10:1-21

- **Summarize:** Summarize the Scripture in your own words.

- **Reflection:** What is God trying to teach you through this passage?

- **Key Verse:** What is the key verse that stands out to you as most important? Write it in the space provided.

- **Action:** What does God want you to do about what you have learned?

quiet time guides

25 five

Topic: Unbelief.

Scripture: John 10:22-42

- **Summarize:** Summarize the Scripture in your own words.

- **Reflection:** What is God trying to teach you through this passage?

- **Key Verse:** What is the key verse that stands out to you as most important? Write it in the space provided.

- **Action:** What does God want you to do about what you have learned?

quiet time guides

26one

Topic: The death of Lazarus.

Scripture: John 11:1-16

- **Summarize:** Summarize the Scripture in your own words.

- **Reflection:** What is God trying to teach you through this passage?

- **Key Verse:** What is the key verse that stands out to you as most important? Write it in the space provided.

- **Action:** What does God want you to do about what you have learned?

quiet time guides

26 *two*

Topic: Comforting sisters.

Scripture: John 11:17-44

- **Summarize:** Summarize the Scripture in your own words.

- **Reflection:** What is God trying to teach you through this passage?

- **Key Verse:** What is the key verse that stands out to you as most important? Write it in the space provided.

- **Action:** What does God want you to do about what you have learned?

quiet time guides

26three

Topic: Prediction.

Scripture: John 12:20-36

- **Summarize:** Summarize the Scripture in your own words.

- **Reflection:** What is God trying to teach you through this passage?

- **Key Verse:** What is the key verse that stands out to you as most important? Write it in the space provided.

- **Action:** What does God want you to do about what you have learned?

quiet time guides

26 four

Topic: More unbelief.

Scripture: John 12:37-50

- **Summarize:** Summarize the Scripture in your own words.

- **Reflection:** What is God trying to teach you through this passage?

- **Key Verse:** What is the key verse that stands out to you as most important? Write it in the space provided.

- **Action:** What does God want you to do about what you have learned?

… quiet time guides

26 five

Topic: Washing feet.

Scripture: John 13:1-17

- **Summarize:** Summarize the Scripture in your own words.

- **Reflection:** What is God trying to teach you through this passage?

- **Key Verse:** What is the key verse that stands out to you as most important? Write it in the space provided.

- **Action:** What does God want you to do about what you have learned?

quiet time guides

27 one

Topic: Betrayal.

Scripture: John 13:18-30

- **Summarize**: Summarize the Scripture in your own words.

- **Reflection**: What is God trying to teach you through this passage?

- **Key Verse**: What is the key verse that stands out to you as most important? Write it in the space provided.

- **Action**: What does God want you to do about what you have learned?

quiet time guides

27 *two*

Topic: Denial.

Scripture: John 13:31-38

- **Summarize:** Summarize the Scripture in your own words.

- **Reflection:** What is God trying to teach you through this passage?

- **Key Verse:** What is the key verse that stands out to you as most important? Write it in the space provided.

- **Action:** What does God want you to do about what you have learned?

quiet time guides

27 three

Topic: The way of the Father.

Scripture: John 14:1-14

- **Summarize:** Summarize the Scripture in your own words.

- **Reflection:** What is God trying to teach you through this passage?

- **Key Verse:** What is the key verse that stands out to you as most important? Write it in the space provided.

- **Action:** What does God want you to do about what you have learned?

the jump journal

quiet time guides

27 four

Topic: Holy Spirit.

Scripture: John 14:15-31

- **Summarize:** Summarize the Scripture in your own words.

- **Reflection:** What is God trying to teach you through this passage?

- **Key Verse:** What is the key verse that stands out to you as most important? Write it in the space provided.

- **Action:** What does God want you to do about what you have learned?

quiet time guides

27 five

Topic: Vine and branches.

Scripture: John 15:1-17

- **Summarize:** Summarize the Scripture in your own words.

- **Reflection:** What is God trying to teach you through this passage?

- **Key Verse:** What is the key verse that stands out to you as most important? Write it in the space provided.

- **Action:** What does God want you to do about what you have learned?

quiet time guides

28one

Topic: Hating disciples.

Scripture: John 15:18 – 16:4

- **Summarize:** Summarize the Scripture in your own words.

- **Reflection:** What is God trying to teach you through this passage?

- **Key Verse:** What is the key verse that stands out to you as most important? Write it in the space provided.

- **Action:** What does God want you to do about what you have learned?

quiet time guides

28 two

Topic: The working Spirit.

Scripture: John 16:5-16

- **Summarize:** Summarize the Scripture in your own words.

- **Reflection:** What is God trying to teach you through this passage?

- **Key Verse:** What is the key verse that stands out to you as most important? Write it in the space provided.

- **Action:** What does God want you to do about what you have learned?

quiet time guides

28 three

Topic: Grief to joy.

Scripture: John 16:17-33

- **Summarize:** Summarize the Scripture in your own words.

- **Reflection:** What is God trying to teach you through this passage?

- **Key Verse:** What is the key verse that stands out to you as most important? Write it in the space provided.

- **Action:** What does God want you to do about what you have learned?

quiet time guides

28 four

Topic: A personal prayer.

Scripture: John 17:1-5

- **Summarize:** Summarize the Scripture in your own words.

- **Reflection:** What is God trying to teach you through this passage?

- **Key Verse:** What is the key verse that stands out to you as most important? Write it in the space provided.

- **Action:** What does God want you to do about what you have learned?

… quiet time guides

28 *five*

Topic: A prayer for disciples. .

Scripture: John 17:6-19

- **Summarize:** Summarize the Scripture in your own words.

- **Reflection:** What is God trying to teach you through this passage?

- **Key Verse:** What is the key verse that stands out to you as most important? Write it in the space provided.

- **Action:** What does God want you to do about what you have learned?

quiet time guides

29 one

Topic: Praying for believers. .

Scripture: John 17:20-26

- **Summarize:** Summarize the Scripture in your own words.

- **Reflection:** What is God trying to teach you through this passage?

- **Key Verse:** What is the key verse that stands out to you as most important? Write it in the space provided.

- **Action:** What does God want you to do about what you have learned?

quiet time guides

29 *two*

Topic: The denials.

Scripture: John 18:12-27

- **Summarize:** Summarize the Scripture in your own words.

- **Reflection:** What is God trying to teach you through this passage?

- **Key Verse:** What is the key verse that stands out to you as most important? Write it in the space provided.

- **Action:** What does God want you to do about what you have learned?

quiet time guides

29 three

Topic: Before Pilate.

Scripture: John 18:28-40

- **Summarize:** Summarize the Scripture in your own words.

- **Reflection:** What is God trying to teach you through this passage?

- **Key Verse:** What is the key verse that stands out to you as most important? Write it in the space provided.

- **Action:** What does God want you to do about what you have learned?

quiet time guides

29 four

Topic: Appearances.

Scripture: John 20:19-31

- **Summarize:** Summarize the Scripture in your own words.

- **Reflection:** What is God trying to teach you through this passage?

- **Key Verse:** What is the key verse that stands out to you as most important? Write it in the space provided.

- **Action:** What does God want you to do about what you have learned?

quiet time guides

29 five

Topic: Reinstatement of a disciple.

Scripture: John 21:15-25

- **Summarize:** Summarize the Scripture in your own words.

- **Reflection:** What is God trying to teach you through this passage?

- **Key Verse:** What is the key verse that stands out to you as most important? Write it in the space provided.

- **Action:** What does God want you to do about what you have learned?

quiet time guides

30 one

Topic: You will be...

Scripture: Acts 1:1-11

- **Summarize:** Summarize the Scripture in your own words.

- **Reflection:** What is God trying to teach you through this passage?

- **Key Verse:** What is the key verse that stands out to you as most important? Write it in the space provided.

- **Action:** What does God want you to do about what you have learned?

quiet time guides

30 *two*

Topic: Addressing the crowd.

Scripture: Acts 2:14-28

- **Summarize:** Summarize the Scripture in your own words.

- **Reflection:** What is God trying to teach you through this passage?

- **Key Verse:** What is the key verse that stands out to you as most important? Write it in the space provided.

- **Action:** What does God want you to do about what you have learned?

quiet time guides

30 three

Topic: The purposes of the church.

Scripture: Acts 2:36-47

- **Summarize:** Summarize the Scripture in your own words.

- **Reflection:** What is God trying to teach you through this passage?

- **Key Verse:** What is the key verse that stands out to you as most important? Write it in the space provided.

- **Action:** What does God want you to do about what you have learned?

quiet time guides

30 four

Topic: Repent.

Scripture: Acts 3:1-26

- **Summarize:** Summarize the Scripture in your own words.

- **Reflection:** What is God trying to teach you through this passage?

- **Key Verse:** What is the key verse that stands out to you as most important? Write it in the space provided.

- **Action:** What does God want you to do about what you have learned?

quiet time guides

30 five

Topic: A prayer and possessions.

Scripture: Acts 4:23-37

- **Summarize:** Summarize the Scripture in your own words.

- **Reflection:** What is God trying to teach you through this passage?

- **Key Verse:** What is the key verse that stands out to you as most important? Write it in the space provided.

- **Action:** What does God want you to do about what you have learned?

quiet time guides

31 one

Topic: Ananias and Sapphira.

Scripture: Acts 5:1-11

- **Summarize:** Summarize the Scripture in your own words.

- **Reflection:** What is God trying to teach you through this passage?

- **Key Verse:** What is the key verse that stands out to you as most important? Write it in the space provided.

- **Action:** What does God want you to do about what you have learned?

quiet time guides

31*two*

Topic: The Ethiopian.

Scripture: Acts 8:26-40

- **Summarize:** Summarize the Scripture in your own words.

- **Reflection:** What is God trying to teach you through this passage?

- **Key Verse:** What is the key verse that stands out to you as most important? Write it in the space provided.

- **Action:** What does God want you to do about what you have learned?

quiet time guides

31 three

Topic: Conversion.

Scripture: Acts 9:1-19; 26:12-18

- **Summarize:** Summarize the Scripture in your own words.

- **Reflection:** What is God trying to teach you through this passage?

- **Key Verse:** What is the key verse that stands out to you as most important? Write it in the space provided.

- **Action:** What does God want you to do about what you have learned?

quiet time guides

31 four

Topic: Cornelius' house.

Scripture: Acts 10:23-48

- **Summarize:** Summarize the Scripture in your own words.

- **Reflection:** What is God trying to teach you through this passage?

- **Key Verse:** What is the key verse that stands out to you as most important? Write it in the space provided.

- **Action:** What does God want you to do about what you have learned?

quiet time guides

31 *five*

Topic: A letter to the Roman Church.

Scripture: Romans 1:1-17

- **Summarize:** Summarize the Scripture in your own words.

- **Reflection:** What is God trying to teach you through this passage?

- **Key Verse:** What is the key verse that stands out to you as most important? Write it in the space provided.

- **Action:** What does God want you to do about what you have learned?

quiet time guides

32 one

Topic: Wrath against man.

Scripture: Romans 1:18-32

- **Summarize:** Summarize the Scripture in your own words.

- **Reflection:** What is God trying to teach you through this passage?

- **Key Verse:** What is the key verse that stands out to you as most important? Write it in the space provided.

- **Action:** What does God want you to do about what you have learned?

quiet time guides

32*two*

Topic: Right judgment.

Scripture: Romans 2:1-16

- **Summarize:** Summarize the Scripture in your own words.

- **Reflection:** What is God trying to teach you through this passage?

- **Key Verse:** What is the key verse that stands out to you as most important? Write it in the space provided.

- **Action:** What does God want you to do about what you have learned?

quiet time guides

32 three

Topic: A faithful God.

Scripture: Romans 3:1-8

- **Summarize:** Summarize the Scripture in your own words.

- **Reflection:** What is God trying to teach you through this passage?

- **Key Verse:** What is the key verse that stands out to you as most important? Write it in the space provided.

- **Action:** What does God want you to do about what you have learned?

quiet time guides

32 four

Topic: None righteous. .

Scripture: Romans 3:9-20

- **Summarize:** Summarize the Scripture in your own words.

- **Reflection:** What is God trying to teach you through this passage?

- **Key Verse:** What is the key verse that stands out to you as most important? Write it in the space provided.

- **Action:** What does God want you to do about what you have learned?

quiet time guides

32 five

Topic: Through faith.

Scripture: Romans 3:21-31

- **Summarize:** Summarize the Scripture in your own words.

- **Reflection:** What is God trying to teach you through this passage?

- **Key Verse:** What is the key verse that stands out to you as most important? Write it in the space provided.

- **Action:** What does God want you to do about what you have learned?

quiet time guides

33 one

Topic: By faith.

Scripture: Romans 4:1-25

- **Summarize:** Summarize the Scripture in your own words.

- **Reflection:** What is God trying to teach you through this passage?

- **Key Verse:** What is the key verse that stands out to you as most important? Write it in the space provided.

- **Action:** What does God want you to do about what you have learned?

quiet time guides

33*two*

Topic: Joy and peace.

Scripture: Romans 5:1-11

- **Summarize:** Summarize the Scripture in your own words.

- **Reflection:** What is God trying to teach you through this passage?

- **Key Verse:** What is the key verse that stands out to you as most important? Write it in the space provided.

- **Action:** What does God want you to do about what you have learned?

quiet time guides

33 three

Topic: Adam and Jesus.

Scripture: Romans 5:12-21

- **Summarize:** Summarize the Scripture in your own words.

- **Reflection:** What is God trying to teach you through this passage?

- **Key Verse:** What is the key verse that stands out to you as most important? Write it in the space provided.

- **Action:** What does God want you to do about what you have learned?

quiet time guides

33 four

Topic: Dead to sin.

Scripture: Romans 6:1-14

- **Summarize:** Summarize the Scripture in your own words.

- **Reflection:** What is God trying to teach you through this passage?

- **Key Verse:** What is the key verse that stands out to you as most important? Write it in the space provided.

- **Action:** What does God want you to do about what you have learned?

quiet time guides

33 five

Topic: A good kind of slave.

Scripture: Romans 6:15-23

- **Summarize:** Summarize the Scripture in your own words.

- **Reflection:** What is God trying to teach you through this passage?

- **Key Verse:** What is the key verse that stands out to you as most important? Write it in the space provided.

- **Action:** What does God want you to do about what you have learned?

quiet time guides

34 one

Topic: Marriage illustration.

Scripture: Romans 7:1-6

- **Summarize:** Summarize the Scripture in your own words.

- **Reflection:** What is God trying to teach you through this passage?

- **Key Verse:** What is the key verse that stands out to you as most important? Write it in the space provided.

- **Action:** What does God want you to do about what you have learned?

quiet time guides

34 two

Topic: Struggling with sin.

Scripture: Romans 7:7-25

- **Summarize:** Summarize the Scripture in your own words.

- **Reflection:** What is God trying to teach you through this passage?

- **Key Verse:** What is the key verse that stands out to you as most important? Write it in the space provided.

- **Action:** What does God want you to do about what you have learned?

quiet time guides

34 three

Topic: The Spirit giving life.

Scripture: Romans 8:1-17

- **Summarize:** Summarize the Scripture in your own words.

- **Reflection:** What is God trying to teach you through this passage?

- **Key Verse:** What is the key verse that stands out to you as most important? Write it in the space provided.

- **Action:** What does God want you to do about what you have learned?

quiet time guides

34 four

Topic: More than conquerors.

Scripture: Romans 8:28-39

- **Summarize:** Summarize the Scripture in your own words.

- **Reflection:** What is God trying to teach you through this passage?

- **Key Verse:** What is the key verse that stands out to you as most important? Write it in the space provided.

- **Action:** What does God want you to do about what you have learned?

quiet time guides

34 five

Topic: God's choice. .

Scripture: Romans 9:1-29

- **Summarize:** Summarize the Scripture in your own words.

- **Reflection:** What is God trying to teach you through this passage?

- **Key Verse:** What is the key verse that stands out to you as most important? Write it in the space provided.

- **Action:** What does God want you to do about what you have learned?

quiet time guides

35one

Topic: Unbelief.

Scripture: Romans 9:30 – 10:21

- **Summarize:** Summarize the Scripture in your own words.

- **Reflection:** What is God trying to teach you through this passage?

- **Key Verse:** What is the key verse that stands out to you as most important? Write it in the space provided.

- **Action:** What does God want you to do about what you have learned?

quiet time guides

35 two

Topic: Branches.

Scripture: Romans 11:11-24

- **Summarize:** Summarize the Scripture in your own words.

- **Reflection:** What is God trying to teach you through this passage?

- **Key Verse:** What is the key verse that stands out to you as most important? Write it in the space provided.

- **Action:** What does God want you to do about what you have learned?

quiet time guides

35 three

Topic: Saving Israel.

Scripture: Romans 11:25-36

- **Summarize:** Summarize the Scripture in your own words.

- **Reflection:** What is God trying to teach you through this passage?

- **Key Verse:** What is the key verse that stands out to you as most important? Write it in the space provided.

- **Action:** What does God want you to do about what you have learned?

quiet time guides

35 four

Topic: Living sacrifices.

Scripture: Romans 12:1-8

- **Summarize:** Summarize the Scripture in your own words.

- **Reflection:** What is God trying to teach you through this passage?

- **Key Verse:** What is the key verse that stands out to you as most important? Write it in the space provided.

- **Action:** What does God want you to do about what you have learned?

quiet time guides

35 five

Topic: A love thing.

Scripture: Romans 12:9-21

- **Summarize:** Summarize the Scripture in your own words.

- **Reflection:** What is God trying to teach you through this passage?

- **Key Verse:** What is the key verse that stands out to you as most important? Write it in the space provided.

- **Action:** What does God want you to do about what you have learned?

quiet time guides

36one

Topic: Authorities.

Scripture: Romans 13:1-7

- **Summarize:** Summarize the Scripture in your own words.

- **Reflection:** What is God trying to teach you through this passage?

- **Key Verse:** What is the key verse that stands out to you as most important? Write it in the space provided.

- **Action:** What does God want you to do about what you have learned?

quiet time guides

36*two*

Topic: A day that's near.

Scripture: Romans 13:8-14

- **Summarize:** Summarize the Scripture in your own words.

- **Reflection:** What is God trying to teach you through this passage?

- **Key Verse:** What is the key verse that stands out to you as most important? Write it in the space provided.

- **Action:** What does God want you to do about what you have learned?

quiet time guides

36three

Topic: Weak and the strong.

Scripture: Romans 14:1-23

- **Summarize:** Summarize the Scripture in your own words.

- **Reflection:** What is God trying to teach you through this passage?

- **Key Verse:** What is the key verse that stands out to you as most important? Write it in the space provided.

- **Action:** What does God want you to do about what you have learned?

quiet time guides

36 four

Topic: Bearing with failings.

Scripture: Romans 15:1-13

- **Summarize:** Summarize the Scripture in your own words.

- **Reflection:** What is God trying to teach you through this passage?

- **Key Verse:** What is the key verse that stands out to you as most important? Write it in the space provided.

- **Action:** What does God want you to do about what you have learned?

quiet time guides

36 five

Topic: Serving God.

Scripture: Romans 15:14-22

- **Summarize:** Summarize the Scripture in your own words.

- **Reflection:** What is God trying to teach you through this passage?

- **Key Verse:** What is the key verse that stands out to you as most important? Write it in the space provided.

- **Action:** What does God want you to do about what you have learned?

quiet time guides

37 one

Topic: Divisions.

Scripture: 1 Corinthians 1:1-17

- **Summarize:** Summarize the Scripture in your own words.

- **Reflection:** What is God trying to teach you through this passage?

- **Key Verse:** What is the key verse that stands out to you as most important? Write it in the space provided.

- **Action:** What does God want you to do about what you have learned?

quiet time guides

37 *two*

Topic: Wisdom and power.

Scripture: 1 Corinthians 1:18 - 2:5

- **Summarize:** Summarize the Scripture in your own words.

- **Reflection:** What is God trying to teach you through this passage?

- **Key Verse:** What is the key verse that stands out to you as most important? Write it in the space provided.

- **Action:** What does God want you to do about what you have learned?

quiet time guides

37 three

Topic: The Spirit gives wisdom.

Scripture: 1 Corinthians 2:6-16

- **Summarize:** Summarize the Scripture in your own words.

- **Reflection:** What is God trying to teach you through this passage?

- **Key Verse:** What is the key verse that stands out to you as most important? Write it in the space provided.

- **Action:** What does God want you to do about what you have learned?

quiet time guides

37 four

Topic: Problems in the body.

Scripture: 1 Corinthians 3:1-23

- **Summarize:** Summarize the Scripture in your own words.

- **Reflection:** What is God trying to teach you through this passage?

- **Key Verse:** What is the key verse that stands out to you as most important? Write it in the space provided.

- **Action:** What does God want you to do about what you have learned?

quiet time guides

37 five

Topic: Apostles. .

Scripture: 1 Corinthians 4:1-21

- **Summarize:** Summarize the Scripture in your own words.

- **Reflection:** What is God trying to teach you through this passage?

- **Key Verse:** What is the key verse that stands out to you as most important? Write it in the space provided.

- **Action:** What does God want you to do about what you have learned?

quiet time guides

38 one

Topic: Dealing with a rouge brother.

Scripture: 1 Corinthians 5:1-13

- **Summarize:** Summarize the Scripture in your own words.

- **Reflection:** What is God trying to teach you through this passage?

- **Key Verse:** What is the key verse that stands out to you as most important? Write it in the space provided.

- **Action:** What does God want you to do about what you have learned?

quiet time guides

38 two

Topic: Sex problems.

Scripture: 1 Corinthians 6:12-20

- **Summarize:** Summarize the Scripture in your own words.

- **Reflection:** What is God trying to teach you through this passage?

- **Key Verse:** What is the key verse that stands out to you as most important? Write it in the space provided.

- **Action:** What does God want you to do about what you have learned?

quiet time guides

38three

Topic: Marriage partners.

Scripture: 1 Corinthians 7:1-40

- **Summarize:** Summarize the Scripture in your own words.

- **Reflection:** What is God trying to teach you through this passage?

- **Key Verse:** What is the key verse that stands out to you as most important? Write it in the space provided.

- **Action:** What does God want you to do about what you have learned?

quiet time guides

38 four

Topic: Exercising freedom.

Scripture: 1 Corinthians 8:1-13

- **Summarize:** Summarize the Scripture in your own words.

- **Reflection:** What is God trying to teach you through this passage?

- **Key Verse:** What is the key verse that stands out to you as most important? Write it in the space provided.

- **Action:** What does God want you to do about what you have learned?

quiet time guides

38 five

Topic: Winning the lost.

Scripture: 1 Corinthians 9:19-27

- **Summarize:** Summarize the Scripture in your own words.

- **Reflection:** What is God trying to teach you through this passage?

- **Key Verse:** What is the key verse that stands out to you as most important? Write it in the space provided.

- **Action:** What does God want you to do about what you have learned?

quiet time guides

39 one

Topic: Believer's freedom.

Scripture: 1 Corinthians 10:23 – 11:1

- **Summarize:** Summarize the Scripture in your own words.

- **Reflection:** What is God trying to teach you through this passage?

- **Key Verse:** What is the key verse that stands out to you as most important? Write it in the space provided.

- **Action:** What does God want you to do about what you have learned?

quiet time guides

39 *two*

Topic: Worship.

Scripture: 1 Corinthians 11:2-16

- **Summarize:** Summarize the Scripture in your own words.

- **Reflection:** What is God trying to teach you through this passage?

- **Key Verse:** What is the key verse that stands out to you as most important? Write it in the space provided.

- **Action:** What does God want you to do about what you have learned?

quiet time guides

39 three

Topic: Lord's Supper.

Scripture: 1 Corinthians 11:17-34

- **Summarize:** Summarize the Scripture in your own words.

- **Reflection:** What is God trying to teach you through this passage?

- **Key Verse:** What is the key verse that stands out to you as most important? Write it in the space provided.

- **Action:** What does God want you to do about what you have learned?

quiet time guides

39 four

Topic: Spiritual gifts.

Scripture: 1 Corinthians 12:1-11

- **Summarize:** Summarize the Scripture in your own words.

- **Reflection:** What is God trying to teach you through this passage?

- **Key Verse:** What is the key verse that stands out to you as most important? Write it in the space provided.

- **Action:** What does God want you to do about what you have learned?

quiet time guides

39 five

Topic: One body.

Scripture: 1 Corinthians 12:12-31

- **Summarize:** Summarize the Scripture in your own words.

- **Reflection:** What is God trying to teach you through this passage?

- **Key Verse:** What is the key verse that stands out to you as most important? Write it in the space provided.

- **Action:** What does God want you to do about what you have learned?

quiet time guides

40 one

Topic: It's about love.

Scripture: 1 Corinthians 13:1-13

- **Summarize:** Summarize the Scripture in your own words.

- **Reflection:** What is God trying to teach you through this passage?

- **Key Verse:** What is the key verse that stands out to you as most important? Write it in the space provided.

- **Action:** What does God want you to do about what you have learned?

quiet time guides

40two

Topic: Resurrection.

Scripture: 1 Corinthians 15:1-11

- **Summarize:** Summarize the Scripture in your own words.

- **Reflection:** What is God trying to teach you through this passage?

- **Key Verse:** What is the key verse that stands out to you as most important? Write it in the space provided.

- **Action:** What does God want you to do about what you have learned?

quiet time guides

40three

Topic: Life again through a man.

Scripture: 1 Corinthians 15:12-34

- **Summarize:** Summarize the Scripture in your own words.

- **Reflection:** What is God trying to teach you through this passage?

- **Key Verse:** What is the key verse that stands out to you as most important? Write it in the space provided.

- **Action:** What does God want you to do about what you have learned?

quiet time guides

40 *four*

Topic: A comforting God.

Scripture: 2 Corinthians 1:1-11

- **Summarize:** Summarize the Scripture in your own words.

- **Reflection:** What is God trying to teach you through this passage?

- **Key Verse:** What is the key verse that stands out to you as most important? Write it in the space provided.

- **Action:** What does God want you to do about what you have learned?

quiet time guides

40 five

Topic: Forgiving sinners.

Scripture: 2 Corinthians 2:5-11

- **Summarize:** Summarize the Scripture in your own words.

- **Reflection:** What is God trying to teach you through this passage?

- **Key Verse:** What is the key verse that stands out to you as most important? Write it in the space provided.

- **Action:** What does God want you to do about what you have learned?

quiet time guides

41 one

Topic: New covenant ministries.

Scripture: 2 Corinthians 2:12 - 3:18

- **Summarize:** Summarize the Scripture in your own words.

- **Reflection:** What is God trying to teach you through this passage?

- **Key Verse:** What is the key verse that stands out to you as most important? Write it in the space provided.

- **Action:** What does God want you to do about what you have learned?

quiet time guides

42 *two*

Topic: Preaching Jesus.

Scripture: 2 Corinthians 4:1-18

- **Summarize**: Summarize the Scripture in your own words.

- **Reflection**: What is God trying to teach you through this passage?

- **Key Verse**: What is the key verse that stands out to you as most important? Write it in the space provided.

- **Action**: What does God want you to do about what you have learned?

quiet time guides

41 three

Topic: An awesome dwelling.

Scripture: 2 Corinthians 5:1-10

- **Summarize:** Summarize the Scripture in your own words.

- **Reflection:** What is God trying to teach you through this passage?

- **Key Verse:** What is the key verse that stands out to you as most important? Write it in the space provided.

- **Action:** What does God want you to do about what you have learned?

quiet time guides

41 four

Topic: Reconciliation ministry.

Scripture: 2 Corinthians 5:11 - 6:2

- **Summarize:** Summarize the Scripture in your own words.

- **Reflection:** What is God trying to teach you through this passage?

- **Key Verse:** What is the key verse that stands out to you as most important? Write it in the space provided.

- **Action:** What does God want you to do about what you have learned?

quiet time guides

41 five

Topic: Hardships.

Scripture: 2 Corinthians 6:3-13

- **Summarize:** Summarize the Scripture in your own words.

- **Reflection:** What is God trying to teach you through this passage?

- **Key Verse:** What is the key verse that stands out to you as most important? Write it in the space provided.

- **Action:** What does God want you to do about what you have learned?

the jump journal

quiet time guides

42 one

Topic: Good yoking.

Scripture: 2 Corinthians 6:14 – 7:1

- **Summarize:** Summarize the Scripture in your own words.

- **Reflection:** What is God trying to teach you through this passage?

- **Key Verse:** What is the key verse that stands out to you as most important? Write it in the space provided.

- **Action:** What does God want you to do about what you have learned?

quiet time guides

42 *two*

Topic: A man's joy.

Scripture: 2 Corinthians 7:2-16

- **Summarize:** Summarize the Scripture in your own words.

- **Reflection:** What is God trying to teach you through this passage?

- **Key Verse:** What is the key verse that stands out to you as most important? Write it in the space provided.

- **Action:** What does God want you to do about what you have learned?

quiet time guides

42three

Topic: Generosity.

Scripture: 2 Corinthians 8:1-15; 9:6-15

- **Summarize:** Summarize the Scripture in your own words.

- **Reflection:** What is God trying to teach you through this passage?

- **Key Verse:** What is the key verse that stands out to you as most important? Write it in the space provided.

- **Action:** What does God want you to do about what you have learned?

quiet time guides

42 four

Topic: Improper measurement.

Scripture: 2 Corinthians 10:1-18

- **Summarize:** Summarize the Scripture in your own words.

- **Reflection:** What is God trying to teach you through this passage?

- **Key Verse:** What is the key verse that stands out to you as most important? Write it in the space provided.

- **Action:** What does God want you to do about what you have learned?

quiet time guides

42 five

Topic: False messengers.

Scripture: 2 Corinthians 11:1-15

- **Summarize**: Summarize the Scripture in your own words.

- **Reflection**: What is God trying to teach you through this passage?

- **Key Verse**: What is the key verse that stands out to you as most important? Write it in the space provided.

- **Action**: What does God want you to do about what you have learned?

quiet time guides

43 one

Topic: Sufferings.

Scripture: 2 Corinthians 11:16-33

- **Summarize:** Summarize the Scripture in your own words.

- **Reflection:** What is God trying to teach you through this passage?

- **Key Verse:** What is the key verse that stands out to you as most important? Write it in the space provided.

- **Action:** What does God want you to do about what you have learned?

quiet time guides

43two

Topic: Thorn.

Scripture: 2 Corinthians 12:1-10

- **Summarize:** Summarize the Scripture in your own words.

- **Reflection:** What is God trying to teach you through this passage?

- **Key Verse:** What is the key verse that stands out to you as most important? Write it in the space provided.

- **Action:** What does God want you to do about what you have learned?

quiet time guides

43 three

Topic: Concern.

Scripture: 2 Corinthians 12:11-21

- **Summarize:** Summarize the Scripture in your own words.

- **Reflection:** What is God trying to teach you through this passage?

- **Key Verse:** What is the key verse that stands out to you as most important? Write it in the space provided.

- **Action:** What does God want you to do about what you have learned?

quiet time guides

43 four

Topic: Warnings.

Scripture: 2 Corinthians 13:1-10

- **Summarize:** Summarize the Scripture in your own words.

- **Reflection:** What is God trying to teach you through this passage?

- **Key Verse:** What is the key verse that stands out to you as most important? Write it in the space provided.

- **Action:** What does God want you to do about what you have learned?

quiet time guides

43 five

Topic: The only Gospel.

Scripture: Galatians 1:6-10

- **Summarize:** Summarize the Scripture in your own words.

- **Reflection:** What is God trying to teach you through this passage?

- **Key Verse:** What is the key verse that stands out to you as most important? Write it in the space provided.

- **Action:** What does God want you to do about what you have learned?

quiet time guides

44 one

Topic: A calling. .

Scripture: Galatians 1:11-24

- **Summarize:** Summarize the Scripture in your own words.

- **Reflection:** What is God trying to teach you through this passage?

- **Key Verse:** What is the key verse that stands out to you as most important? Write it in the space provided.

- **Action:** What does God want you to do about what you have learned?

quiet time guides

44 *two*

Topic: Accepted.

Scripture: Galatians 2:1-10

- **Summarize:** Summarize the Scripture in your own words.

- **Reflection:** What is God trying to teach you through this passage?

- **Key Verse:** What is the key verse that stands out to you as most important? Write it in the space provided.

- **Action:** What does God want you to do about what you have learned?

quiet time guides

44 three

Topic: Christ lives in me.

Scripture: Galatians 2:11-21

- **Summarize:** Summarize the Scripture in your own words.

- **Reflection:** What is God trying to teach you through this passage?

- **Key Verse:** What is the key verse that stands out to you as most important? Write it in the space provided.

- **Action:** What does God want you to do about what you have learned?

the jump journal

quiet time guides

44 *four*

Topic: Faith vs. Laws.

Scripture: Galatians 3:1-14

- **Summarize:** Summarize the Scripture in your own words.

- **Reflection:** What is God trying to teach you through this passage?

- **Key Verse:** What is the key verse that stands out to you as most important? Write it in the space provided.

- **Action:** What does God want you to do about what you have learned?

quiet time guides

44 five

Topic: The promise.

Scripture: Galatians 3:15-25

- **Summarize:** Summarize the Scripture in your own words.

- **Reflection:** What is God trying to teach you through this passage?

- **Key Verse:** What is the key verse that stands out to you as most important? Write it in the space provided.

- **Action:** What does God want you to do about what you have learned?

quiet time guides

45 one

Topic: Sons of God.

Scripture: Galatians 3:26 - 4:7

- **Summarize:** Summarize the Scripture in your own words.

- **Reflection:** What is God trying to teach you through this passage?

- **Key Verse:** What is the key verse that stands out to you as most important? Write it in the space provided.

- **Action:** What does God want you to do about what you have learned?

quiet time guides

45two

Topic: More concern.

Scripture: Galatians 4:8-20

- **Summarize:** Summarize the Scripture in your own words.

- **Reflection:** What is God trying to teach you through this passage?

- **Key Verse:** What is the key verse that stands out to you as most important? Write it in the space provided.

- **Action:** What does God want you to do about what you have learned?

quiet time guides

45three

Topic: Freedom in Christ.

Scripture: Galatians 5:1-15

- **Summarize:** Summarize the Scripture in your own words.

- **Reflection:** What is God trying to teach you through this passage?

- **Key Verse:** What is the key verse that stands out to you as most important? Write it in the space provided.

- **Action:** What does God want you to do about what you have learned?

quiet time guides

45 four

Topic: The Spirit gives life.

Scripture: Galatians 5:16-26

- **Summarize:** Summarize the Scripture in your own words.

- **Reflection:** What is God trying to teach you through this passage?

- **Key Verse:** What is the key verse that stands out to you as most important? Write it in the space provided.

- **Action:** What does God want you to do about what you have learned?

quiet time guides

45 five

Topic: Doing good.

Scripture: Galatians 6:1-10

- **Summarize:** Summarize the Scripture in your own words.

- **Reflection:** What is God trying to teach you through this passage?

- **Key Verse:** What is the key verse that stands out to you as most important? Write it in the space provided.

- **Action:** What does God want you to do about what you have learned?

quiet time guides

46 one

Topic: A new creation.

Scripture: Galatians 6:11-18

- **Summarize:** Summarize the Scripture in your own words.

- **Reflection:** What is God trying to teach you through this passage?

- **Key Verse:** What is the key verse that stands out to you as most important? Write it in the space provided.

- **Action:** What does God want you to do about what you have learned?

quiet time guides

46 two

Topic: Spiritual blessings.

Scripture: Ephesians 1:3-14

- **Summarize:** Summarize the Scripture in your own words.

- **Reflection:** What is God trying to teach you through this passage?

- **Key Verse:** What is the key verse that stands out to you as most important? Write it in the space provided.

- **Action:** What does God want you to do about what you have learned?

quiet time guides

46three

Topic: Prayer and thanksgiving.

Scripture: Ephesians 1:15-23

- **Summarize:** Summarize the Scripture in your own words.

- **Reflection:** What is God trying to teach you through this passage?

- **Key Verse:** What is the key verse that stands out to you as most important? Write it in the space provided.

- **Action:** What does God want you to do about what you have learned?

quiet time guides

46 four

Topic: Alive in Christ.

Scripture: Ephesians 2:1-10

- **Summarize:** Summarize the Scripture in your own words.

- **Reflection:** What is God trying to teach you through this passage?

- **Key Verse:** What is the key verse that stands out to you as most important? Write it in the space provided.

- **Action:** What does God want you to do about what you have learned?

quiet time guides

46 five

Topic: One in Christ.

Scripture: Ephesians 2:11-22

- **Summarize:** Summarize the Scripture in your own words.

- **Reflection:** What is God trying to teach you through this passage?

- **Key Verse:** What is the key verse that stands out to you as most important? Write it in the space provided.

- **Action:** What does God want you to do about what you have learned?

quiet time guides

47 one

Topic: Preaching.

Scripture: Ephesians 3:1-13

- **Summarize:** Summarize the Scripture in your own words.

- **Reflection:** What is God trying to teach you through this passage?

- **Key Verse:** What is the key verse that stands out to you as most important? Write it in the space provided.

- **Action:** What does God want you to do about what you have learned?

quiet time guides

47 *two*

Topic: Praying.

Scripture: Ephesians 3:14-21

- **Summarize:** Summarize the Scripture in your own words.

- **Reflection:** What is God trying to teach you through this passage?

- **Key Verse:** What is the key verse that stands out to you as most important? Write it in the space provided.

- **Action:** What does God want you to do about what you have learned?

quiet time guides

47 three

Topic: Unified.

Scripture: Ephesians 4:1-16

- **Summarize:** Summarize the Scripture in your own words.

- **Reflection:** What is God trying to teach you through this passage?

- **Key Verse:** What is the key verse that stands out to you as most important? Write it in the space provided.

- **Action:** What does God want you to do about what you have learned?

quiet time guides

47 four

Topic: Children of the light.

Scripture: Ephesians 4:17-32

- **Summarize:** Summarize the Scripture in your own words.

- **Reflection:** What is God trying to teach you through this passage?

- **Key Verse:** What is the key verse that stands out to you as most important? Write it in the space provided.

- **Action:** What does God want you to do about what you have learned?

quiet time guides

47 five

Topic: Imitators.

Scripture: Ephesians 5:1-21

- **Summarize:** Summarize the Scripture in your own words.

- **Reflection:** What is God trying to teach you through this passage?

- **Key Verse:** What is the key verse that stands out to you as most important? Write it in the space provided.

- **Action:** What does God want you to do about what you have learned?

quiet time guides

48 one

Topic: Family matters.

Scripture: Ephesians 5:22 - 6:4

- **Summarize:** Summarize the Scripture in your own words.

- **Reflection:** What is God trying to teach you through this passage?

- **Key Verse:** What is the key verse that stands out to you as most important? Write it in the space provided.

- **Action:** What does God want you to do about what you have learned?

quiet time guides

48 two

Topic: Armor.

Scripture: Ephesians 6:10-20

- **Summarize:** Summarize the Scripture in your own words.

- **Reflection:** What is God trying to teach you through this passage?

- **Key Verse:** What is the key verse that stands out to you as most important? Write it in the space provided.

- **Action:** What does God want you to do about what you have learned?

quiet time guides

48 three

Topic: Feelings and prayer.

Scripture: Philippians 1:1-11

- **Summarize:** Summarize the Scripture in your own words.

- **Reflection:** What is God trying to teach you through this passage?

- **Key Verse:** What is the key verse that stands out to you as most important? Write it in the space provided.

- **Action:** What does God want you to do about what you have learned?

quiet time guides

48 four

Topic: Advancing the Gospel.

Scripture: Philippians 1:12-30

- **Summarize:** Summarize the Scripture in your own words.

- **Reflection:** What is God trying to teach you through this passage?

- **Key Verse:** What is the key verse that stands out to you as most important? Write it in the space provided.

- **Action:** What does God want you to do about what you have learned?

quiet time guides

48 five

Topic: Humility.

Scripture: Philippians 2:1-11

- **Summarize:** Summarize the Scripture in your own words.

- **Reflection:** What is God trying to teach you through this passage?

- **Key Verse:** What is the key verse that stands out to you as most important? Write it in the space provided.

- **Action:** What does God want you to do about what you have learned?

quiet time guides

49 one

Topic: Shining.

Scripture: Philippians 2:12-18

- **Summarize:** Summarize the Scripture in your own words.

- **Reflection:** What is God trying to teach you through this passage?

- **Key Verse:** What is the key verse that stands out to you as most important? Write it in the space provided.

- **Action:** What does God want you to do about what you have learned?

quiet time guides

49 *two*

Topic: Flesh problems.

Scripture: Philippians 3:1-11

- **Summarize:** Summarize the Scripture in your own words.

- **Reflection:** What is God trying to teach you through this passage?

- **Key Verse:** What is the key verse that stands out to you as most important? Write it in the space provided.

- **Action:** What does God want you to do about what you have learned?

quiet time guides

49 three

Topic: Pressing on.

Scripture: Philippians 3:12 - 4:1

- **Summarize:** Summarize the Scripture in your own words.

- **Reflection:** What is God trying to teach you through this passage?

- **Key Verse:** What is the key verse that stands out to you as most important? Write it in the space provided.

- **Action:** What does God want you to do about what you have learned?

quiet time guides

49 four

Topic: God's strength.

Scripture: Philippians 4:10-20

- **Summarize:** Summarize the Scripture in your own words.

- **Reflection:** What is God trying to teach you through this passage?

- **Key Verse:** What is the key verse that stands out to you as most important? Write it in the space provided.

- **Action:** What does God want you to do about what you have learned?

quiet time guides

49 five

Topic: Always thanking.

Scripture: Colossians 1:1-14

- **Summarize:** Summarize the Scripture in your own words.

- **Reflection:** What is God trying to teach you through this passage?

- **Key Verse:** What is the key verse that stands out to you as most important? Write it in the space provided.

- **Action:** What does God want you to do about what you have learned?

quiet time guides

51one

Topic: The Supreme Christ.

Scripture: Colossians 1:15-23

- **Summarize:** Summarize the Scripture in your own words.

- **Reflection:** What is God trying to teach you through this passage?

- **Key Verse:** What is the key verse that stands out to you as most important? Write it in the space provided.

- **Action:** What does God want you to do about what you have learned?

quiet time guides

50 two

Topic: Laboring for Christ.

Scripture: Colossians 1:24-29

- **Summarize:** Summarize the Scripture in your own words.

- **Reflection:** What is God trying to teach you through this passage?

- **Key Verse:** What is the key verse that stands out to you as most important? Write it in the space provided.

- **Action:** What does God want you to do about what you have learned?

quiet time guides

50three

Topic: Encouraging the heart.

Scripture: Colossians 2:1-5

- **Summarize:** Summarize the Scripture in your own words.

- **Reflection:** What is God trying to teach you through this passage?

- **Key Verse:** What is the key verse that stands out to you as most important? Write it in the space provided.

- **Action:** What does God want you to do about what you have learned?

quiet time guides

54 four

Topic: Freedom.

Scripture: Colossians 2:6-23

- **Summarize:** Summarize the Scripture in your own words.

- **Reflection:** What is God trying to teach you through this passage?

- **Key Verse:** What is the key verse that stands out to you as most important? Write it in the space provided.

- **Action:** What does God want you to do about what you have learned?

quiet time guides

50 five

Topic: Holy living rules.

Scripture: Colossians 3:1-17

- **Summarize:** Summarize the Scripture in your own words.

- **Reflection:** What is God trying to teach you through this passage?

- **Key Verse:** What is the key verse that stands out to you as most important? Write it in the space provided.

- **Action:** What does God want you to do about what you have learned?

quiet time guides

51 one

Topic: Imitators.

Scripture: 1 Thessalonians 1:1-10

- **Summarize:** Summarize the Scripture in your own words.

- **Reflection:** What is God trying to teach you through this passage?

- **Key Verse:** What is the key verse that stands out to you as most important? Write it in the space provided.

- **Action:** What does God want you to do about what you have learned?

quiet time guides

51 *two*

Topic: Paul's ministry.

Scripture: 1 Thessalonians 2:1-16

- **Summarize**: Summarize the Scripture in your own words.

- **Reflection**: What is God trying to teach you through this passage?

- **Key Verse**: What is the key verse that stands out to you as most important? Write it in the space provided.

- **Action**: What does God want you to do about what you have learned?

quiet time guides

51 three

Topic: Longing.

Scripture: 1 Thessalonians 2:17 – 3:5

- **Summarize:** Summarize the Scripture in your own words.

- **Reflection:** What is God trying to teach you through this passage?

- **Key Verse:** What is the key verse that stands out to you as most important? Write it in the space provided.

- **Action:** What does God want you to do about what you have learned?

quiet time guides

51 four

Topic: An encouraging report.

Scripture: 1 Thessalonians 3:6-13

- **Summarize:** Summarize the Scripture in your own words.

- **Reflection:** What is God trying to teach you through this passage?

- **Key Verse:** What is the key verse that stands out to you as most important? Write it in the space provided.

- **Action:** What does God want you to do about what you have learned?

quiet time guides

51 *five*

Topic: Living for pleasing.

Scripture: 1 Thessalonians 4:1-12

- **Summarize:** Summarize the Scripture in your own words.

- **Reflection:** What is God trying to teach you through this passage?

- **Key Verse:** What is the key verse that stands out to you as most important? Write it in the space provided.

- **Action:** What does God want you to do about what you have learned?

quiet time guides

52 one

Topic: A thief in the night.

Scripture: 1 Thessalonians 4:13 - 5:11

- **Summarize:** Summarize the Scripture in your own words.

- **Reflection:** What is God trying to teach you through this passage?

- **Key Verse:** What is the key verse that stands out to you as most important? Write it in the space provided.

- **Action:** What does God want you to do about what you have learned?

quiet time guides

52*two*

Topic: The Spirit's fire.

Scripture: 1 Thessalonians 5:12-28

- **Summarize:** Summarize the Scripture in your own words.

- **Reflection:** What is God trying to teach you through this passage?

- **Key Verse:** What is the key verse that stands out to you as most important? Write it in the space provided.

- **Action:** What does God want you to do about what you have learned?

quiet time guides

52 three

Topic: Counted worthy

Scripture: 2 Thessalonians 1:1-12

- **Summarize:** Summarize the Scripture in your own words.

- **Reflection:** What is God trying to teach you through this passage?

- **Key Verse:** What is the key verse that stands out to you as most important? Write it in the space provided.

- **Action:** What does God want you to do about what you have learned?

quiet time guides

52 four

Topic: Law breaking and standing firm.

Scripture: 2 Thessalonians 2:1-17

- **Summarize:** Summarize the Scripture in your own words.

- **Reflection:** What is God trying to teach you through this passage?

- **Key Verse:** What is the key verse that stands out to you as most important? Write it in the space provided.

- **Action:** What does God want you to do about what you have learned?

quiet time guides

52 five

Topic: Prayer and idleness.

Scripture: 2 Thessalonians 3:1-15

- **Summarize:** Summarize the Scripture in your own words.

- **Reflection:** What is God trying to teach you through this passage?

- **Key Verse:** What is the key verse that stands out to you as most important? Write it in the space provided.

- **Action:** What does God want you to do about what you have learned?

group takeaway

the jump journal

group takeaway

1

Theme:

Scripture:

Key Truths:

How This Connects To Me:

Actions To Take:

group takeaway

2

Theme:

Scripture:

Key Truths:

How This Connects To Me:

Actions To Take:

group takeaway

3

Theme:

Scripture:

Key Truths:

How This Connects To Me:

Actions To Take:

group takeaway

4

Theme:

Scripture:

Key Truths:

How This Connects To Me:

Actions To Take:

group takeaway

5

Theme:

Scripture:

Key Truths:

How This Connects To Me:

Actions To Take:

group takeaway

6

Theme:

Scripture:

Key Truths:

How This Connects To Me:

Actions To Take:

group takeaway

7

Theme:

Scripture:

Key Truths:

How This Connects To Me:

Actions To Take:

group takeaway

8

Theme:

Scripture:

Key Truths:

How This Connects To Me:

Actions To Take:

group takeaway

9

Theme:

Scripture:

Key Truths:

How This Connects To Me:

Actions To Take:

group takeaway

10

Theme:

Scripture:

Key Truths:

How This Connects To Me:

Actions To Take:

11

group takeaway

Theme:

Scripture:

Key Truths:

How This Connects To Me:

Actions To Take:

the jump journal

group takeaway

12

Theme:

Scripture:

Key Truths:

How This Connects To Me:

Actions To Take:

group takeaway

13

Theme:

Scripture:

Key Truths:

How This Connects To Me:

Actions To Take:

group takeaway

14

Theme:

Scripture:

Key Truths:

How This Connects To Me:

Actions To Take:

15

group takeaway

Theme:

Scripture:

Key Truths:

How This Connects To Me:

Actions To Take:

group takeaway

16

Theme:

Scripture:

Key Truths:

How This Connects To Me:

Actions To Take:

group takeaway

17

Theme:

Scripture:

Key Truths:

How This Connects To Me:

Actions To Take:

group takeaway

18

Theme:

Scripture:

Key Truths:

How This Connects To Me:

Actions To Take:

19

group takeaway

Theme:

Scripture:

Key Truths:

How This Connects To Me:

Actions To Take:

group takeaway

20

Theme:

Scripture:

Key Truths:

How This Connects To Me:

Actions To Take:

group takeaway

21

Theme:

Scripture:

Key Truths:

How This Connects To Me:

Actions To Take:

group takeaway

22

Theme:

Scripture:

Key Truths:

How This Connects To Me:

Actions To Take:

group takeaway

23

Theme:

Scripture:

Key Truths:

How This Connects To Me:

Actions To Take:

group takeaway

24

Theme:

Scripture:

Key Truths:

How This Connects To Me:

Actions To Take:

25 group takeaway

Theme:

Scripture:

Key Truths:

How This Connects To Me:

Actions To Take:

group takeaway

26

Theme:

Scripture:

Key Truths:

How This Connects To Me:

Actions To Take:

the jump journal

group takeaway

27

Theme:

Scripture:

Key Truths:

How This Connects To Me:

Actions To Take:

group takeaway

28

Theme:

Scripture:

Key Truths:

How This Connects To Me:

Actions To Take:

29

group takeaway

Theme:

Scripture:

Key Truths:

How This Connects To Me:

Actions To Take:

group takeaway

30

Theme:

Scripture:

Key Truths:

How This Connects To Me:

Actions To Take:

31 group takeaway

Theme:

Scripture:

Key Truths:

How This Connects To Me:

Actions To Take:

group takeaway

32

Theme:

Scripture:

Key Truths:

How This Connects To Me:

Actions To Take:

group takeaway

33

Theme:

Scripture:

Key Truths:

How This Connects To Me:

Actions To Take:

group takeaway

34

Theme:

Scripture:

Key Truths:

How This Connects To Me:

Actions To Take:

group takeaway

35

Theme:

Scripture:

Key Truths:

How This Connects To Me:

Actions To Take:

group takeaway

36

Theme:

Scripture:

Key Truths:

How This Connects To Me:

Actions To Take:

group takeaway

37

Theme:

Scripture:

Key Truths:

How This Connects To Me:

Actions To Take:

group takeaway

38

Theme:

Scripture:

Key Truths:

How This Connects To Me:

Actions To Take:

group takeaway

39

Theme:

Scripture:

Key Truths:

How This Connects To Me:

Actions To Take:

40

group takeaway

Theme:

Scripture:

Key Truths:

How This Connects To Me:

Actions To Take:

41 group takeaway

Theme:

Scripture:

Key Truths:

How This Connects To Me:

Actions To Take:

group takeaway

42

Theme:

Scripture:

Key Truths:

How This Connects To Me:

Actions To Take:

the jump journal

group takeaway

43

Theme:

Scripture:

Key Truths:

How This Connects To Me:

Actions To Take:

group takeaway

44

Theme:

Scripture:

Key Truths:

How This Connects To Me:

Actions To Take:

the jump journal

45

group takeaway

Theme:

Scripture:

Key Truths:

How This Connects To Me:

Actions To Take:

group takeaway

46

Theme:

Scripture:

Key Truths:

How This Connects To Me:

Actions To Take:

47

group takeaway

Theme:

Scripture:

Key Truths:

How This Connects To Me:

Actions To Take:

the jump journal

group takeaway

48

Theme:

Scripture:

Key Truths:

How This Connects To Me:

Actions To Take:

the jump journal

group takeaway

49

Theme:

Scripture:

Key Truths:

How This Connects To Me:

Actions To Take:

group takeaway

50

Theme:

Scripture:

Key Truths:

How This Connects To Me:

Actions To Take:

group takeaway

51

Theme:

Scripture:

Key Truths:

How This Connects To Me:

Actions To Take:

group takeaway

52

Theme:

Scripture:

Key Truths:

How This Connects To Me:

Actions To Take:

worship takeaway

the jump journal

worship takeaway

1

Theme:

Scripture:

Key Truths:

How This Connects To Me:

Actions To Take:

worship takeaway

2

Theme:

Scripture:

Key Truths:

How This Connects To Me:

Actions To Take:

worship takeaway

3

Theme:

Scripture:

Key Truths:

How This Connects To Me:

Actions To Take:

worship takeaway

♃

Theme:

Scripture:

Key Truths:

How This Connects To Me:

Actions To Take:

worship takeaway

5

Theme:

Scripture:

Key Truths:

How This Connects To Me:

Actions To Take:

worship takeaway

6

Theme:

Scripture:

Key Truths:

How This Connects To Me:

Actions To Take:

… # worship takeaway

7

Theme:

Scripture:

Key Truths:

How This Connects To Me:

Actions To Take:

worship takeaway

8

Theme:

Scripture:

Key Truths:

How This Connects To Me:

Actions To Take:

worship takeaway

9

Theme:

Scripture:

Key Truths:

How This Connects To Me:

Actions To Take:

worship takeaway

10

Theme:

Scripture:

Key Truths:

How This Connects To Me:

Actions To Take:

11

worship takeaway

Theme:

Scripture:

Key Truths:

How This Connects To Me:

Actions To Take:

worship takeaway

12

Theme:

Scripture:

Key Truths:

How This Connects To Me:

Actions To Take:

the jump journal

worship takeaway

13

Theme:

Scripture:

Key Truths:

How This Connects To Me:

Actions To Take:

worship takeaway 14

Theme:

Scripture:

Key Truths:

How This Connects To Me:

Actions To Take:

the jump journal

15
worship takeaway

Theme:

Scripture:

Key Truths:

How This Connects To Me:

Actions To Take:

worship takeaway
16

Theme:

Scripture:

Key Truths:

How This Connects To Me:

Actions To Take:

worship takeaway

17

Theme:

Scripture:

Key Truths:

How This Connects To Me:

Actions To Take:

worship takeaway

18

Theme:

Scripture:

Key Truths:

How This Connects To Me:

Actions To Take:

the jump journal
344

# 19

worship takeaway

Theme:

Scripture:

Key Truths:

How This Connects To Me:

Actions To Take:

worship takeaway

20

Theme:

Scripture:

Key Truths:

How This Connects To Me:

Actions To Take:

21

worship takeaway

Theme:

Scripture:

Key Truths:

How This Connects To Me:

Actions To Take:

worship takeaway

22

Theme:

Scripture:

Key Truths:

How This Connects To Me:

Actions To Take:

23

worship takeaway

Theme:

Scripture:

Key Truths:

How This Connects To Me:

Actions To Take:

worship takeaway

24

Theme:

Scripture:

Key Truths:

How This Connects To Me:

Actions To Take:

25

worship takeaway

Theme:

Scripture:

Key Truths:

How This Connects To Me:

Actions To Take:

worship takeaway

26

Theme:

Scripture:

Key Truths:

How This Connects To Me:

Actions To Take:

worship takeaway

27

Theme:

Scripture:

Key Truths:

How This Connects To Me:

Actions To Take:

worship takeaway

28

Theme:

Scripture:

Key Truths:

How This Connects To Me:

Actions To Take:

worship takeaway

29

Theme:

Scripture:

Key Truths:

How This Connects To Me:

Actions To Take:

worship takeaway

30

Theme:

Scripture:

Key Truths:

How This Connects To Me:

Actions To Take:

31

worship takeaway

Theme:

Scripture:

Key Truths:

How This Connects To Me:

Actions To Take:

worship takeaway

32

Theme:

Scripture:

Key Truths:

How This Connects To Me:

Actions To Take:

… # worship takeaway

33

Theme:

Scripture:

Key Truths:

How This Connects To Me:

Actions To Take:

worship takeaway

34

Theme:

Scripture:

Key Truths:

How This Connects To Me:

Actions To Take:

35

worship takeaway

Theme:

Scripture:

Key Truths:

How This Connects To Me:

Actions To Take:

worship takeaway

36

Theme:

Scripture:

Key Truths:

How This Connects To Me:

Actions To Take:

worship takeaway

37

Theme:

Scripture:

Key Truths:

How This Connects To Me:

Actions To Take:

worship takeaway

38

Theme:

Scripture:

Key Truths:

How This Connects To Me:

Actions To Take:

worship takeaway

39

Theme:

Scripture:

Key Truths:

How This Connects To Me:

Actions To Take:

the jump journal

worship takeaway

40

Theme:

Scripture:

Key Truths:

How This Connects To Me:

Actions To Take:

worship takeaway

41

Theme:

Scripture:

Key Truths:

How This Connects To Me:

Actions To Take:

worship takeaway

42

Theme:

Scripture:

Key Truths:

How This Connects To Me:

Actions To Take:

worship takeaway

43

Theme:

Scripture:

Key Truths:

How This Connects To Me:

Actions To Take:

worship takeaway

44

Theme:

Scripture:

Key Truths:

How This Connects To Me:

Actions To Take:

worship takeaway

45

Theme:

Scripture:

Key Truths:

How This Connects To Me:

Actions To Take:

worship takeaway

46

Theme:

Scripture:

Key Truths:

How This Connects To Me:

Actions To Take:

the jump journal

worship takeaway

47

Theme:

Scripture:

Key Truths:

How This Connects To Me:

Actions To Take:

worship takeaway

48

Theme:

Scripture:

Key Truths:

How This Connects To Me:

Actions To Take:

worship takeaway

49

Theme:

Scripture:

Key Truths:

How This Connects To Me:

Actions To Take:

worship takeaway

50

Theme:

Scripture:

Key Truths:

How This Connects To Me:

Actions To Take:

51

worship takeaway

Theme:

Scripture:

Key Truths:

How This Connects To Me:

Actions To Take:

worship takeaway

52

Theme:

Scripture:

Key Truths:

How This Connects To Me:

Actions To Take:

calendar

the jump journal

calendar

january

february

march

april

the jump journal

calendar

may

june

july

august

the jump journal

calendar

september

october

november

december

the jump journal

www.ingramcontent.com/pod-product-compliance
Lightning Source LLC
Chambersburg PA
CBHW060451090426
42735CB00011B/1967